WHAT'S HER WILD

WHAT'S HER WILD

AN UNTOLD STORY

Andraya Grangroth

BOOKLOGIX®
Alpharetta, Georgia

The author has tried to recreate events, locations, and conversations from her memories of them. In some instances, in order to maintain their anonymity, the author has changed the names of individuals and places. She may also have changed some identifying characteristics and details such as physical attributes, occupations, and places of residence.

Copyright © 2023 by Andraya Grangroth

All rights reserved. No part of this book may be reproduced or transmitted in any form or by any means, electronic or mechanical, including photocopying, recording, or any information storage and retrieval system, without permission in writing from the author.

ISBN: 978-1-6653-0688-1 - Paperback
eISBN: 978-1-6653-0689-8 - eBook

These ISBNs are the property of BookLogix for the express purpose of sales and distribution of this title. The content of this book is the property of the copyright holder only. BookLogix does not hold any ownership of the content of this book and is not liable in any way for the materials contained within. The views and opinions expressed in this book are the property of the Author/Copyright holder, and do not necessarily reflect those of BookLogix.

∞This paper meets the requirements of ANSI/NISO Z39.48-1992 (Permanence of Paper)

Photography by Andraya Grangroth.
Description on back of the book by Sean McGowan.
Facts and scripture quoted by http://www.llchurch.org.

082923

CONTENTS

Prologue   *vii*

PART ONE

Chapter One	3
Chapter Two	7
Chapter Three	11
Chapter Four	15
Chapter Five	19
Chapter Six	23
Chapter Seven	27
Chapter Eight	29
Chapter Nine	33
Chapter Ten	39
Chapter Eleven	43
Chapter Twelve	47
Chapter Thirteen	51
Chapter Fourteen	55
Chapter Fifteen	59

PART TWO

Chapter Sixteen	65
Chapter Seventeen	69
Chapter Eighteen	73
Chapter Nineteen	81
Chapter Twenty	89
Chapter Twenty-One	95
Chapter Twenty-Two	101
Chapter Twenty-Three	105
Chapter Twenty-Four	115

Chapter Twenty-Five	123
Chapter Twenty-Six	135
Chapter Twenty-Seven	141
Chapter Twenty-Eight	147
Chapter Twenty-Nine	151
Chapter Thirty	155
Chapter Thirty-One	161
Chapter Thirty-Two	169

PART THREE

Chapter Thirty-Three	175
Chapter Thirty-Four	177
Chapter Thirty-Five	183
Acknowledgments	*187*

PROLOGUE

The lodge was buzzing with excitement and anticipation for opening day, as clients played pool and shared hunting stories. Traveling far, these clients would spend Thanksgiving with us during their five-day hunt.

Walking into the lodge, I instantly saw that everyone was getting along fine, the energy positive and hopeful. As the lead guide I oversaw giving the welcome and safety speech to our clients and what to expect during the next five days as they hunted elk and mule deer. At the end of the speech, I asked the clients if they wanted to participate in a pool, simply where the clients put in however much money and whoever shot the first elk would take home the cash. Twenty-dollar bills were pulled from their pockets and wallets as I went into one of our cabins to retrieve an envelope for the pool money, and in doing so I stumbled upon the *Colorado Hunter* magazine in which I was featured.

The article on me was titled "Not Just a Huntress" and it talked about my connection with hunting, how it became my ultimate healer, and how as a woman I was paving my way in the hunting industry. Like finding a hidden treasure, I was excited to find it in the dusty cabin and brought it back into the lodge to show Tom, the cook, what I had found.

"Attention, attention! Gentlemen, your lead guide is right here in this magazine! Come take a look! This is your lead guide!" Tom shouted from the kitchen, making sure everyone in the lodge heard.

Tom was like a brother to me, and he was the first person to jump in and show me the ropes when I first started at Timber Bench Outfitters. Most of the guys in camp did a quick look over the article, not really reading but skimming. No surprise there, as I feel like there is a lack of reading anything on paper these days.

Feeling a tap on my shoulder, I turned around and "C," one

of our clients, was holding the magazine close to his chest when he asked me, "Do you have another copy of this? I would love to take it home to my wife." I told him I didn't, but I was more than happy to pass this magazine along.

Taking a big gulp of my coffee from my thermos, I, accompanied by C, bounced as the jeep drove over ruts and rocks on our way to the morning stand. Typically, the conversations that would happen on the first morning driving out to the stand covered the surface area—where are you from, do you have kids, are you married, how many years have you been a guide, etc. But no conversation like that happened this morning.

"You know, Draya, I read your article last night and I need to tell you something. I'm sorry if this gets too personal, and if it does, then tell me to shut the fuck up. Anyway, I wanted to tell you how proud of you I am for being so brave to tell your story about being sexually abused in a magazine. In a place for the world to see." Then, C informed me, "You know, the same thing happened to my two boys." C went on to tell me about how his two boys were molested when they were just five years old, and how it happened by their babysitter in their own home. He told me about how one of his sons has moved on and healed, but how the other one still struggles with it.

I wanted so badly in that moment to hug his boys, now men, and to tell them that I knew the feeling and that life would continue for the better. Obviously, that wasn't possible, but I found a silver lining in this conversation with C. Ever since I started my journey of healing, I'd felt a desire to share with the world my story, and perhaps in doing so, I would inspire someone along the way.

As I headed back to the lodge after dropping C off at this stand, my path ahead of me was clear—it was time to write this book you hold in your hand now.

As you read, you'll learn about the tools I have found to help with self-healing. I want to tell you about the fucked-up shit that goes on behind too many doors, and about the fear bred in church pews. I want to tell you about the emotional and spiritual connection I have found through hunting and how it's not just about the photo of you behind a big set of antlers. I want to talk about all that I have experienced and how it has changed my life for the better. Please note if you have suffered trauma to proceed with caution as stories from my past may bring up triggers from yours.

Buckle up, grab a tissue, and enjoy.

PART ONE

CHAPTER ONE

It was the summer of July 2003. I was 12 years of age as my sister, just a year older than me, and I picked weeds from the garden. The sun was hot on our necks as we bent over working the land. The rule was you had to weed two rows before going off to play for the day. As the sweat dripped from our foreheads, we couldn't wait to throw on our swimsuits and head to the creek about a mile away from the house.

Finishing my two rows before my sister, I jumped in to help her, our eager hands working fast as dust filled our nostrils. Grasshoppers jumped about, occasionally landing on our arms as we worked. The dogs would lay nearby, soaking up the sun and keeping a watch over everyone, a buzzing property of sustainability.

Throwing the last of the weeds into the bucket, we ran across the yard to put on our swimsuits that were hanging on the clothesline. We yelled to Mom that we were finished and headed to the creek to swim. Grabbing our towels and tossing on our tennis shoes, we ran out the door.

The trail down to the creek consisted of blackberry bushes, stinging nettle, and other various weeds in which we would try our best to create a trail with the machete. Regardless of how much we chopped down, there was always one of us who would get stung, but that never slowed us down, as the small red bumps would soon fade and no longer itch. As we approached the creek, we could hear it roar in the background. Reaching the final descent, we made our way down a muddy hillside, using the roots as steps and holding onto a small fir tree to avoid tumbling down the hill. The last obstacle was to jump across a small side channel of the creek, and then we would finally get to cool off.

Tossing our towels on the mossy rocks and slipping out of our shoes, we were ready to swim, and one by one we jumped in. Coal Creek was no small creek, and looking back, it surprises me that our parents trusted us to swim there without an adult. Waterfalls flowed into big deep pools of water, creating the perfect swimming holes, and rocks covered in dark green moss made for the best slides. A giant fir tree had fallen, creating a platform on which we would jump off; quickly crawling back up out of the water scared the crawdads would nip at our toes. Some days we even brought lunch meat, which we would dangle from the end of a stick, luring in the crawdads from their hiding spots under the rocks. Once they got close to the surface, we would grab behind their pinchers and toss them into a bucket.

We explored the waterfalls and climbed across them, jumping into the bubbly cold water below. The smooth rock that was exposed from the river became eroded in spots, which created little pockets of water that would hold crawdads, water bugs, and small shells attached to the rock. When I was too young to swim in the bigger pools, that is where I would play; my life jacket held me tight just in case I fell in. Hours would go by as we splashed about, and the world around us seemed to fade away. Soon the hot sun was gone behind the tall evergreens, the water was no longer enticing, and with a full bucket of crawdads, we headed back up the hill for an afternoon feast.

A sparkling night sky held our gaze as we looked up, curled up in our sleeping bags. My skin was hot from the day's sunburn, and we talked about what adventure we'd go on tomorrow. Sounds of frogs would cricket from the backyard pond, and a pack of coyotes would howl from the hillside behind the house. Bats would fly above our heads, snacking on bugs, and our dogs would curl up at our feet. I always felt safe sleeping outside. Truth be told, I felt more safe sleeping under the stars than I did in my own bedroom.

As a young child, I spent every second I could outside, even after it was dark out. I looked forward to summer, knowing I would be able to sleep outside, escaping the nightmares I would regularly have when sleeping in my own bed. Many nights, I would wake as I gasped for breath, grabbing at my throat, and dripping with sweat. My heart would beat loud and fast in my chest as I started to cry into my pillow. Often, I would look over at the door, cringing at what or who might be in the doorway, and relief would come over me as I realized it was just a nightmare. Several times as a young girl, I even peed on the carpet in the corner of my room, too scared to leave the bedroom to use the bathroom during the night.

I was held hostage by the fear of who was in that dark hallway. Would *he* be waiting for me in the dark too? Looking up into the depths of the Milky Way, I was able to escape those terrifying nightmares, fading into a deep sleep as the crickets sang their nightly songs.

Throughout this book, I'll share stories of connection that bring proof that nature is the ultimate healer. Please remember as you read or listen, this is *my* story. I am not trying to tell you how to live your life or how to heal from traumatic moments, but perhaps my journey will allow you to expand your mind on what is possible and bring awareness to this crazy world.

At the age of thirty-two, I feel as though I have lived many lifetimes. I have been reborn over and over; I have found the ultimate success. All of this is possible because of my opportunist mind-set. The success I have found is not that of money or a white picket-fence yard; rather, it's quite the opposite. The riches I possess are not that of materialistic goods but of the relationships I have found and the memories that leave a mark within me.

As I share my story with you, my intentions are not to place shame or point fingers. This is much bigger than that and I hope you're inspired along the way. You are capable of love, of your dream career, of happiness, of anything you desire. It's up to you to get it done, and I know you can.

CHAPTER TWO

Three of us five sisters piled in the bathroom, washing, drying, and curling our hair. Sundays were for worship and a day of rest. With our hair done up and dress clothes on, we headed out the door to the church up on the hill. Hopping out of the van, I saw a friend on the far side of the parking lot and ran over. "Want to play tag?" someone would ask. And there we would go, running our wiggles out before having to sit for two hours during church.

Even as a kid I dreaded having to sit through the sermons and would often pass notes with my friends to keep myself from falling asleep. Many times, Mom or Dad would flick us on the back of the head, insinuating we needed to be quiet and listen. Each Sunday would consist of two opening hymns, followed by a sermon, another hymn, another sermon, then two more closing hymns. The minister would read a passage from the Bible and then go into deep detail on how this was how we should live our life.

Our day-to-day life revolved around this religion called Laestadian Lutheran Christianity (LLC), a religious movement—its teachings based on the Bible and Lutheran Confessions. On June 9, 1973, the organization was named the Association of American Laestadian Congregations (AALC) before the association changed its name in 1994 to better convey its spiritual heritage. As of 2016, the Laestadian Lutheran Church has thirty-three member congregations in the United States and Canada, with the highest concentrations of members in Minnesota, Washington, Arizona, and Michigan.

In the United States and Saskatchewan, Canada the congregations are served by ninety ministers, nearly all of them lay preachers. The main teaching among them is Jesus's suffering, death, and resurrection. The work of Jesus Christ continues in this world as the work of the Holy Spirit. The Laestadian Lutheran Church teaches about God's kingdom and the need for repentance and the forgiveness of sins. The church holds, in accord with the Lutheran Confessions, that the Bible is the highest guide and authority for the Christian faith, doctrine, and life. The norms in the congregation—such as refraining from birth control, make-up, and dancing—are some of the things members do not feel are right to do as a child of God.

No birth control, make-up, or dancing are only a few restrictions we had growing up. We weren't allowed to participate in sports nor could we spend time with "unbelievers" (those who weren't Laestadian) outside of school or work. There was no television or movies in the house, and any music with a beat was prohibited. There was no altering of our appearance in any way, and we dressed very modestly. Sex was to be saved for marriage, and dating was taken very seriously, as you only dated someone with the intention to marry them. Life growing up was very sheltered, but as a child I, along with everyone else, believed the words the minister preached, and every night before bed we would ask our parents to forgive our sins, that way if we died in our sleep we would go to heaven.

The LLC mission, according to LLChurch.org, is, "To preach the gospel of repentance and remission of sins to the people of our communities, our nations, and throughout the world so that they might become partakers with us of the grace that God offers sin-fallen man in His Son Jesus Christ. To nurture and strengthen the faith of the believing and root our children in Christian faith in God's kingdom. To awaken and inspire Christian values and ethics, soberness of mind, love of homeland, and responsible citizenship among the people of our nations." The forgiveness of sins growing up was essentially a getaway-free card. Anytime you sinned, you were encouraged to ask for it to be forgiven, even if it was seventy times a day. Once that sin was forgiven it was washed away in the sea of grace, never to be spoken of again. They instructed you to never shy away from asking, because if you desired to have your sins forgiven, that meant you still had the Holy Spirit.

One summer day, I was hungry, so I picked an apple from the tree and was going up the stairs to my room when my dad saw me with the apple.

"Did you ask if you can have that?" his stern voice questioned me.

"No," I replied, timid and scared of getting spanked for not asking.

"Well . . . what do you need to do?" he instructed me.

"Can I have my sins forgiven?" I asked with my head down, the apple down at my side. And so, he forgave me, and we went on with our day. There were nights as a kid when I would forget to ask for my sins to be forgiven and would lay awake all night, fearing sleep. I was so afraid to fall asleep because my brain was conditioned to believe that if I fell asleep without my sins forgiven, and I happened to die in my sleep, then I would burn in hell for eternity. The ministers would preach upon us, saying that if we died without hearing the gospel, instead of going to heaven, we would burn in hell, feeling every ounce of flame forever. There would be no peaceful death. You would suffer forever for your actions. What kind of God allows that? Let me tell you, believing that and living up to that message—that messes you up as a kid, and I can say that because, personally, I know.

Along with Sunday morning worship, children would attend Sunday School. Preschoolers would color pictures of Jesus and angels, and as you got a little older, the lessons became more serious. Once you got to middle school, they had us memorizing the Lord's Prayer, the Benediction, and the Ten Commandments.

Every Saturday night I sat somewhere in the house, my catechism in my hand as I read the message over and over. As I lay in bed reciting it over and over, my anxiety went through the roof, feeling an immense pressure to ingrain the message into my memory just like they asked of us. "Remember the Sabbath to keep it holy," "Thou shalt not have any other gods before me," and "Thou shalt not take the name of the Lord thy God in vain," are a few I somehow remember. And there in class, standing in front of our classmates, we would recite the message of the week.

CHAPTER THREE

You may be sensing my distaste for my religious upbringing, but there was a lot of good that came from my childhood. Growing up in a family with fourteen children, nine brothers and four sisters, made for always having a playmate, and there was always someone teasing someone. We lived on a beautiful and fruitful ten acres of land, in Longview, Washington. Living in the western part of the state, there was no shortage of rain, as we saw roughly three hundred days of it a year.

The summer weather was perfect for growing fruits and vegetables, and that we did. In our garden, we harvested corn, potatoes, zucchini, carrots, beets, tomatoes, squash, rhubarb, green beans, and onions. Apple, pear, and cherry trees were scattered throughout the property, along with rows of strawberry, raspberry, and blueberry bushes and even grape vines on an old wooden fence. Blackberries grew wild and were considered a weed with how quickly they took over anything in their path.

My sister and I loved grabbing gallon ice cream buckets and going to pick blackberries, our fingers stained dark purple from the juices. We would feast as we picked our way through the many tunnels in the vines, inevitably getting scratched by the thorns.

Many summer days, I would wander out to the garden and pick a handful of green beans, or a squash, and cook them up for lunch and gather fresh berries for a smoothie on those hot days. The garden hose was close by, and I still remember the taste of half-rinsed carrots, munching on them with still a little bit of dirt in their creases.

There was always dirt under our nails, and in the summer our feet became so callused, we could run across the gravel driveway as if we had shoes on.

My mom loved to garden, and she created the most beautiful flower beds I have ever seen. They wrapped around the front yard and the entire house. She would organize them so perfectly and beautifully, creating beds of colorful plants, shrubs, and ferns. The property was surrounded by them, creating a pedestal that our house seemed to sit on. A home filled with love, adventure, and hard work. The front lawn was my mom's baby, as she only allowed the push mower to cut the grass. Every other day she would lace up her tennis shoes, fill the tank, and cut the grass in such perfect lines that it looked as if it was a golf course. Mom's place was either in the kitchen or out kneeling by the flower beds. I now understand that her gardening was what kept her sane—being a mother of fourteen and having to take care of all of us and the home couldn't have been easy.

Located in the center of the property was my dad's shop. It was filled with various wood-cutting tools and a giant meat hook on which we would hang the elk and deer we harvested. The lawnmowers, wheelbarrows, and other tools filled up the dimly lit space in the back. Dad was always building something and had stashes of different wood lined up against one of the walls. Our cats would often have their kittens upstairs among the antiques that collected dust.

Located next to the shop was our pond that each one of us kids helped build. Days were spent hauling small rocks to line the pond's floor, and then bigger ones to create flower beds to surround them. Flowers and grasses of all types brought a vibrant glow, seeming to draw visitors to the pond, and the gravel path that went around created a romantic feel. Waterfalls flowed into both ponds and a small bridge went over the small stream that trickled into the lower one. An old wooden bench swing brought up the back corner and many hours were spent slowly swinging, watching the many birds and insects that thrived off the plants. It was a work of art and often Mom and Dad would sip their evening coffee enjoying their masterpiece.

Along with the vegetable garden and fruit trees, we also had chickens, turkeys, sheep, a horse, a ram, cats, and dogs on the property. We would collect the eggs daily from the chicken coop, and once a year, we would butcher a few of them to feed our growing family. Raising chickens and turkeys gave us a deep connection with where our meat came from as young as we could remember.

On butcher days, we would gather the turkeys or chickens into a small pen, and one by one as we caught them, Dad would cut their heads off with a big machete. Bright red blood squirted out as the bird ran in circles, as if it was doing its last dance. No meat was ruined in this method of taking, allowing us to use every bit of organic meat we had raised. After the bird was done with its death dance, we would quickly grab it, pulling out the feathers so Mom could then gut it. It was a team effort process to fill our bellies with some of the best meat out there.

I remember these moments so vividly—my family working together, everyone in tune with their place, their job, some were bloody, and some were covered in feathers. This was simply our way of life. To some of you, this may seem cruel and inhumane, but when is the last time you saw where your meat came from?

CHAPTER FOUR

During the summer months, Dad would take us kids down to the Columbia River to fish for salmon and steelhead. We would wake up at four a.m. and make the drive west toward the fishing spots Dad had found over the years. One day, it was just Dad and I fishing at a local spot we called "the bum hole." Old scraggly men with big beer bellies would show up with their beer cans and fishing poles, and it wasn't long until they passed out drunk in their chairs, a pile of empty beer cans on the ground next to their feet. Disgusted, Dad was eager to find a new place for him and his young daughter to fish, and at low tide, a bend upriver from us exposed itself. Pointing, Dad told me, "That looks like good fishing over there. Let's go drop a line and see if anything bites."

We walked along the wet rocky shore, and I tried my best not to fall on my face, my rubber boots not offering much support or traction. We tied on our shrimp, tossed the line out, and within minutes the pole started to bounce, and the bell attached started to ring, letting us know we had a fish on. We worked as a team as I grabbed the pole and Dad grabbed the net. I set the hook, and the fight between the fish and I began.

The steelhead swam quickly upriver, causing the tip of my rod to fall.

"Keep that tip up, keep the line tight!" Dad reminded me as he stood next to the river's edge. My heart raced and my arms shook as I did my best to keep the fish on the line. I slowly reeled the rod down, then pulled it up. I did this over and over, keeping the line tight. Finally, my arms tired and shaky, I reeled the fish right into the net that Dad held.

Upon netting the fish, we discovered it was a keeper. Its back adipose fin was sliced off, meaning it went through the fish hatchery. Fish with a back fin not snipped off were called "wild" fish, only for the Indians to keep. Excited about our new spot and the quick catch, we threw the line back out. Within the next couple hours, Dad and I both limited out with two beautiful steelheads each—a great start to a new fishing spot.

As we started our trek up the hill, I carried the fish sack on my back, while Dad carried the rest of the tackle. The trail was steep and we soon realized it was covered in poison oak—there was no way we would be able to get up without getting covered in red itchy bumps that would burn for days. As we backtracked along the rocky shoreline I could see a smirk on my dad's face.

"I think we should name that spot 'Buoy Five.'" Dad said. A red and white buoy bounced about on the choppy river telling the ships which channel to use, and now it was also directing us to a small piece of heaven along the river. Little did we know at the time that this spot would provide a space for our family to spend quality time together, for our nieces and nephews to learn how to put food on the table, and that sometimes you'd lose the fish but regardless you would keep trying.

Buoy Five became a place I couldn't live without, as I spent most of my teenage summers there. I loved being by the water, watching the different tides, feeling the warm sun on my skin, and hearing the constant splash of small waves hitting the rocky beach. It brought a much-needed calm to my racing mind, and I felt safe as I waited for the fish to bite.

With each summer, Buoy Five would build more character. One morning upon arriving, we noticed something along the shoreline—it was an old fishing net. Grabbing it, we tied some string to the ends and then tied it up between two big trees, creating a hammock in the shade of a big maple. We built a ladder that connected the river bottom to the washed-out hillside. With each fish we caught, we cut out a slot in the ladder, a scoreboard on how many fish we had caught there. A rope swing hung from another big maple that the nieces and nephews were often pushed on.

Soon we had the entire family at the new fishing hole, and Mom would start the day by making breakfast of pancakes, bacon, and eggs with fresh coffee. Dad never wandered too far from his old aluminum chair where he constantly tied fresh bait. I loved watching him in his zone. He was in his happy place. Frankly, we all were in our happy place. There were no cares in the world except catching fish and enjoying the playground Mother Earth had to offer. Big cargo ships would cruise by causing big waves to crash along the shore, and eagles would soar above keeping an eye on the catch we had laying in a small stream, to keep fresh in the summer sun.

Most anglers along the river would just fish the morning incoming tide, but we found great success in fishing all day long, many times catching fish during the middle of the day. I loved being by the river and learning about the fish. The skill of living a sustainable life and knowing where my food came from was created in those moments, and I'm forever grateful I was raised this way. As the warm afternoon sun started to settle in the west, often the sky would become bright orange, reflecting on the river, and making it look like flowing lava. We had caught our limit for the day, and it was time to head home. I tossed the heavy canvas bag full of fish over my shoulder and started up the steep hill to the truck. Even then, I was obsessed with carrying the heavy weight on my back up a mountain. I loved the challenge, and it made the taste of the fish we ate that much sweeter.

There was plenty of work to still be done after we got home. Dad would fillet the fish and my job was to pull out the bones, rinse, and vacuum seal the meat. Oftentimes, we would enjoy a late-night dinner of fresh salmon with potatoes, carrots, and onions from the garden. Our dog Katie would sit beside my dad at the grill waiting for juicy strips of fish. The thing is, none of this ever felt like work, it was just what we did—and I loved every step of it.

CHAPTER FIVE

For just a few years growing up, we had an old brown mustang horse named Tinker. I loved spending time with Tinker and would spend hours in his stall, grooming or feeding him grain. I would talk to him and cry, and he would listen, emotions in his dark brown eyes. He made me feel calm and safe.

I wanted to learn how to ride him, so my brother offered to teach me. He showed me how to saddle him and how to attach his bridle and reins. Helping to hoist me up into the saddle one day, we made our way through the field and into the timber that brought us to an old logging road just behind our house. After a little while, my brother let me take full control of the reins as he held on near the bridle just in case Tinker got any funny ideas. I was surprised at how quickly and smoothly Tinker moved, and soon we were a couple of miles behind the house, far from anyone's eyes or ears.

Reaching a dip in the road hidden from view, my brother abruptly stopped Tinker and climbed up on the back of the saddle behind me.

Confused I asked him, "What are you doing?"

Saying nothing (or so that's what I remember) his rough hands made their way under and up my shirt to my small breasts. I flinched from his touch, and he grabbed onto me, holding me down to the saddle, reassuring me that it was going to be okay, and that he was just curious. Soon his hands unbuttoned and unzipped my jeans. I wanted to throw up as I felt the blood leave my face.

"You're becoming a woman, Andraya, you're getting pubic hair," he whispered in my ear.

Chills went down my spine, and once again I flinched from his touch. I looked around the forest hoping someone was out for a walk. I needed a miracle to escape, and so I closed my eyes and prayed. Feeling his fingers work their way into my pants, I nearly threw up as he proceeded to play with my clitoris. I was consumed by fear—fear of what would happen if I ran or if I screamed. I had fallen victim to his nasty actions, and we were miles away from help. I struggle to remember the details of what happened next and how long it lasted. I assume it was my body's natural way of trying to survive a traumatic experience such as this, resulting in me blacking out.

The cabin was dark and musty smelling as flies buzzed around the only small window. There was a wood fireplace in the corner and a twin-sized bed pushed up against the wall. I couldn't remember how I got there as I heard the door shut behind me. The sound of my brother's pants unzipping sent another round of chills through me, and he told me to pull my pants down and bend over.

Fear overcame me and for a second, I wanted to run but was compelled to do as he said.

"Just breathe and relax," he told me.

I could feel his breath on the back of my neck now and I knew it was too late—I was trapped. This wasn't the first time he had touched me, but this was definitely the worst of it.

"Looks like you're becoming a woman, Andraya, you're getting little boobs," my brother whispered in my ear, as if that would help me relax.

I wanted to run, I wanted to kick him in the nuts, I wanted to spit in his face, punch him, slap him, but I couldn't move. His legs spread wide behind me, and his forearms held strong at my side against the bed frame, trapping me in.

A sharp pain coursed through my body as his dick slammed into my vagina. There was no foreplay, he just wanted his fix and be done. Tears rolled down my cheeks as I bit my lip, holding in the screams of pain and anger.

I've tried so hard over the years to remember more details from these traumatic moments, but I can't bring myself to find clarity on what happened next. How long did he rape me? Did he come? At one point, did I finally find the strength and courage to run to safety? How did I allow myself to be alone with him again? What I remember next is sitting on the shower floor, the hot water on my back, my knees tucked into my chest as I wept and screamed. I had filled a washcloth with soap and scrubbed until my skin turned red, trying to wash away all the disgusting acts he had just played out on me. I was ashamed of myself for allowing him to take advantage of me. I was ashamed of myself for I should have known better than to be alone with him. *This was all my fault*, I told myself. *I did this, not him.*

A few days later was Sunday, and as the minister gave his sermon, I actually paid attention, unlike most Sundays. I looked around at the men sitting in the pew, their hands folded, their arms around their wives, and I questioned if what happened to me was a normal thing. I was so young, naïve, and so confused.

"You can believe all your sins forgiven, in Jesus's name and precious blood. These sins are washed away in the sea of grace forever, just as long as you believe," the minister preached. Others around me wiped tears from their cheeks as the following scene played out: The minister's arm reached out, his hand flat as he recited, "Believe all sins, all sins forgiven, in Jesus's name and blood, in Jesus's name, believe all sins, all sins forgiven in Jesus's name and precious blood . . ." Over and over, the minister preached these words as the lost souls in the pews requested them, their hands raised in the air as if they needed to hear this message directly to believe it.

As I took in these words from the man behind the pulpit, my brainwashed mind told me I would be okay. My brother's horrible actions were forgiven, and so was I. I could forget about it, I could move on—that's what the minister was telling me and that's what the Bible tells us. If I chose to not forget this sin, I would then be sinning, and as believers, we must strive to live with a clean conscience. I decided on that day, sitting in the pew, that I would never tell anyone, for why would I if my brother's actions were forgiven and washed away forever? Now my existence became that of: *how do I survive?*

And survive I did. For nearly fifteen years, I held this secret in. It was easier to forget about it, to stash it away in a place I never thought I'd visit again. The trauma I held inside me would and did cause low self-esteem, a lack of confidence, terrifying nightmares, not being able to regulate my emotions, sudden mood changes, fear of being in my own home—the list goes on.

It wasn't until years down the road that I snapped back to reality. It took hearing another victim's story for the awful memory of my brother sexually abusing me to resurface. I often wonder if or when I would have remembered these horrid events if she hadn't publicly told her truth.

CHAPTER SIX

As soon as I was twelve years old, I enrolled in a hunter safety class. This consisted of three days of classroom work, where we discussed the basics of what it means to be a hunter. The topics ranged from gun safety to identifying animals, identifying tracks and scat, rules and regulations, conservation, scenarios in the field, and safety, ending with a written test on the third day and followed up with a final test in the field.

We met in the back room of Bob's Sporting Goods. My best friend Amanda and I were the only girls in the class, and we were just as, if not more, eager to learn as the boys were. This hunter safety course was something I had been looking forward to ever since I tagged along on my first hunt with my dad at around ten years old. I would walk behind him in the woods, stepping in his tracks as I intently watched his every move, soaking it all in like a sponge. My brothers would come home from a hunt and hang their deer or elk upside down in our shop, and there, too, I was in awe of the process of it all. I was amazed at how they so naturally and smoothly cut away prime cuts from the animal, leaving nothing behind but the carcass. I couldn't wait until I was old enough to join them.

After three long days of classroom work, it was time for our field test. Amanda and I were giddy with excitement, already looking forward to future hunts together. The field test was a boot-on-the-ground-style test where we had to hike through the forest, safely carrying our weapons. With each fence or steam crossing, we would open the action of our weapon and make sure the gun's safety was on as we handed it to our partner and crossed over. If that wasn't done correctly, you wouldn't pass; thus, we secured that we understood how important safety is in the field.

At the end of our hike through the forest was our final test. We had to pick the correct ammunition from a variety of bullets piled up on the tailgate, load the weapon, and then shoot it. If we did all that correctly and safely, we passed. I passed with flying colors and the countdown to next year's hunting season had begun.

It was a rainy fall day, and I nearly ran up the driveway from the bus, for all I could think about was getting out for an evening stand sit. This rainy weather would give me an advantage as I snuck through the woods looking for a black-tailed buck. I had homework that day just like most, but it would have to wait until after dark.

Throwing on fleece pants and a hoodie from one of our many totes of hunting clothes, I slipped on my rubber boots and yelled to Mom, "I'm headed for the corner of the field to hunt. I'll be back at dark!" A three-acre parcel of our land was made up of fir trees, and in the back corner was a patch of a small group of maple trees. Surrounding the outside of this parcel was a thick forest, the ground foliage making it nearly impossible to navigate through. If something did travel through there, it was obvious, as there would be a trail or tunnel.

I decided to sit against one of the small firs closest to the thick timber, and as I sat and waited, the rain softly drizzled. The small tree gave me limited protection from the rain, but it didn't bother me, as I was laser-focused on being still and listening. My dad's sweet sixteen gauge sat in my lap, loaded and ready to go. The day was nearing its end, and it was almost dark when I heard a stick break. In return, I called back using my doe bleat call.

Raising my knees, I settled my elbows on them and hugged the shotgun snug to my shoulder. Within seconds, a two-by-two buck stepped out, his chest held high and his tongue licking his lips. I breathed slowly, steadying my heart rate as I waited for him to turn broadside. The buck fed for a bit but was focused on the doe call he just heard. He was fifteen yards away now, perfectly broadside and totally unaware I was about to kill him. I slowly pulled the trigger, and he kicked his back hooves up in the air and ran to the trees. I popped open the barrel and grabbed the slug casing, still smoking. Throwing it in my pocket, I ran for the house to tell Dad. *I can't believe it; I just shot my first buck, and I did it all on my own!*

Running through the entranceway of the kitchen, I saw everyone was just finishing up dinner and starting to clean up. Dad was in his usual spot at the head of the table, relaxed in his chair, clearly satisfied with the meal Mom just served.

"I shot a buck!" I exclaimed, my voice high with excitement.

"No, you're just messing with me," my dad responds.

I pulled the empty slug from my wet pocket and held it out in front me, my hand still shaking with adrenaline.

"Well, it looks like we've got some work to do," Dad said as he pushed his chair back from the kitchen table. Grabbing headlamps and the key to the tractor, we headed to the shop so Dad could drive the tractor to where the buck died.

Seeing the buck in the headlights, Dad jumped out and gave me a big hug and a high five as the biggest grin covered his face. "I'm proud," he told me as he hugged me again. We took photos and soaked in the moment of my first harvest.

Scooping the buck up in the bucket of the tractor, we drove it back to the shop and hung it from the meat hook. I intently watched as Dad grabbed the garbage bin and placed it under the buck. As he sliced away at the fur and lining on its stomach, the guts started to fall out, landing in the bucket with a splat.

"Want to help skin him?" Dad asked me. Nearly jumping out of my boots, I took hold of the knife, and after years of watching, I finally got to do my part. As we cut away the hide, beautiful dark organic meat, tendons, and fat wrapped around the bones of this majestic wild animal. My family would eat well, and I was honored to harvest this elusive deer for them.

As the years went on, my father and I spent many days in the field, scouting and hunting, and long summer days on the river, just the two of us. There was an unspoken bond we shared as we explored wild places, and I would soak it all in watching his every move. Looking back at these moments in time, I've come to realize my dad was my true hero, as he provided me the space to feel free among the chaos of my mind. As we climbed mountains or sat quietly along the river, I felt a connection with something that was so much bigger than the message the minister would preach from behind the pulpit. During those years, my father instilled the passion I have for hunting within me, and for that, I am forever grateful.

CHAPTER SEVEN

Every summer growing up, from ages seven to fifteen, we would attend a summer camp called Youth Camp. Youth Camp was five days long, located at Millersylvania State Park in Washington. There were roughly eighty students and twenty staff members who would gather for a week of studying the Bible and the catechism and to rejoice in singing from the songs and hymns of Zion. There was limited time for play as the studies were to be taken very seriously.

The girls had girl cabins and the boys had boy cabins. These cabins were on opposite sides of the property, far away from any temptation. Each of us had a "big" who oversaw a certain cabin and a group of kids. Outside of the main lodge, next to the American flag, was a giant bell. Anytime that bell rang, we needed to report to the main lodge.

Every morning the bell would ring for breakfast, and before you knew it, the lodge was buzzing full of kids, taking their seats so we could all join in for morning hymns and thanks before being excused to go eat. There was a full kitchen staff, typically all ladies, who made sure our bellies were full every day and night.

We were on a strict schedule at camp, starting with an early breakfast followed by morning devotion, then a lesson, then free time, then lunch, followed by more lessons, some free time, dinner, then evening devotion or discussion, and then the best part, skits!

Being the entertainer, I was always in charge of coming up with skits and finding people who wanted to participate in them. Naturally, I've always been a people person and could talk to anyone who walked in the room. I used this attention as a coping mechanism. It gave me validation that I was worthy of people's time, and if I was making other people laugh, then nobody asked questions and nobody knew I was sad. Whether it was at Youth Camp, a family reunion, or when I got older and started to attend the adult camps, I was always the one who oversaw the entertainment. I made myself as goofy as possible and people would often cry from laughing so hard. It made me feel good knowing I could make others happy, and I would soak in their energy, soon forgetting I was feeling depressed, and the anxiety would fade away.

The most vivid memories I have from these camps are of swimming and canoeing in the lake and playing volleyball or capture the flag in the big field. With our Finnish ethnicity, we were born athletes, and there was always some sport being played. Basketball, volleyball, football, kickball—you name it, and we played it. It's funny knowing we were not allowed to play sports in school but that's exactly what we did when we gathered as young kids.

Filing into the lodge, we found our seats each day and quietly listened as an adult spoke on various topics related to being a child of God. Doodling and daydreaming, I never paid much attention to what they were saying. Honestly, there never was a time in my life that I felt a true connection to the words they spoke. I never had that spiritual connection; I was just going with the motions of being a child of God. The students I sat beside during these camps felt more like strangers than they did friends. There seemed to be a disconnect between us, and perhaps that was just me building walls to protect myself.

I've always wondered why I never told anyone, especially my girlfriends, about my abuse. Conversations seemed to only cover the surface area as we learned from our parents to not talk about difficult things. Surely something they, too, learned from their parents. A generational issue that I am sure still plays on today.

CHAPTER EIGHT

I was home alone when I heard someone at the front door. Looking out the kitchen windows, I saw a man getting out of his old beat-up truck. He had a black mask on and was wearing a dark blue sweatshirt with his hood up—and he was holding a knife in his hand. Finding a place to hide quickly between the china cabinet and the wall, I folded my arms across my chest and tried my hardest to slow my breathing.

I could hear the intruder slowly open the front door, the hardwood floor in the entryway creaking under his feet as he made his way to the kitchen. The footsteps were getting closer, and I knew if he entered the dining room, he would see me and I would be cornered, so I bolted. I ran for the living room door that led to the backyard. Everything seemed to move in slow motion, but eventually, I made it to the door. Nearly tripping down the wooden stairs, I could see my exit route: the forest behind the house. I knew every hiding spot, every trail, every thick patch of brush, and I headed for it, but I couldn't seem to run fast enough.

Looking back, I saw the man, with his giant knife clenched in his hand, his long strides gaining ground on me. As I turned my head to face forward, I tripped over my own two feet and fell to the ground. I landed hard in the grass, and just as I tried to push up, he was on top of me.

His breath smelled of evil and his big strong body was no match for mine. I fought back, my fist swinging wildly, my legs kicking, but I was no match for the giant man. I screamed for help knowing someone must be around to hear, but nobody came. The madman screamed as if he was a Viking going into battle, the blade of his knife held up high above him, celebrating his victory before he took another life.

There was no pain, just the sound of a blade slicing the flesh on my throat, followed by the sound of blood gushing like that of a garden hose. The light faded away as my body fell to the grass, and all was black.

Gasping for breath, I jolted awake, my throat dry and my neck sore. Reality set in that I was okay and safe, and as I looked at the bedroom door, relief flooded over me as I realized it was just another nightmare. I pulled the blankets up close to my face and hugged my "blankey" that I'd had since I was a baby. Tears rolled down my cheeks as my breathing was heavy and my heart raced. I so badly wanted a drink of water, but I was terrified to leave the bedroom, terrified of what was waiting in the dark. The rest of the night, I fought sleep, fearing what would happen next.

The following night, the same nightmare happened but this time instead of falling in the grass, I made it to the forest. Knowing where the trail was that would bring me to the road below, I took it to gain ground from the evil man chasing me.

I crossed the road and ran up to our neighbor's front door, my fist banging hard as I yelled, "HELP! OPEN! HELP!" My heart was beating out of my chest as I looked back in hopes I had lost the man. I continued to bang on the door, but nobody opened it, and there on the neighbor's front step, once again my throat was slit, with no feeling of pain, just the sound.

Jolting awake, in a full sweat this time, I gasped for breath and grabbed at my throat. Looking over at my sister, she was fast asleep next to me. I lay back down, my hand on my chest feeling my pounding heart, and I silently cried myself back to sleep.

This next nightmare is blurry in details except for the man's face and the location. I was in the basement of the church when this man cornered me in the hallway to the bathrooms. Right there in the church, he pulled my pants down and raped me. The freakiest part of this nightmare was that this man did time behind bars for molesting his own daughter. This man was a Sunday school teacher and would often touch/wrestle the girls in my grade, a smirk on his face as he did so. Young and naïve, I didn't think anything about it then. I wish I could have seen the signs; I wish I was educated on what was right and wrong. These conversations never came up in my home. We never talked about the human body, sexuality, puberty, and how it changes with age. We never talked about sex and our body's desires, as sex was to be saved for marriage so why would we talk about it? I often wonder, if my parents had these conversations with us, would my brother have raped me? Could this all have been prevented?

If you're reading this and you have children, I beg you, *please* talk to your children about all the things my parents didn't talk to me about, and start when they are young, that way things will happen naturally. These conversations shouldn't be something we shy away from. Nobody, absolutely nobody, deserves to go through what I and many others have gone through. This doesn't mean things won't happen, but the more we educate and spread awareness on these issues, the safer our community, schools, churches, and homes will be.

These were just a couple of the nightmares that seemed to be on repeat, and as I grew older, they traveled with me wherever I went. The day after a night filled with them, I wanted nothing more but to escape to the forest and breathe in the fresh air and feel the breeze on my skin. The nausea held me at bay and conversation with anyone was far from possible.

I would walk through the hallways of the high school, crossing my arms over my chest, my head down, as I would frequently look over my shoulder. I would go through the motion of the day feeling that at any second my nightmares would come to life. The clock would slowly tick onward and the thought of falling back to sleep had me running to the toilet and throwing up, as if I was trying to remove the trauma from within me. My head felt like a jackhammer was busy at work and any quick movements of my eyes would only intensify the pain.

I avoided telling anyone about these nightmares, as I told myself over and over they were just dreams, we all have them. I had become a master of survival, my mind strong in convincing myself I was okay. I was my own worst enemy, fighting a battle alone that could never be won, and for fifteen years, this was my purpose.

The chains that bound me were locked tight around my wrist and I was the one who held the key. Fear held me captive—fear of what would happen if I released myself from them—and so I kept my secret hidden deep within, and the chains remained locked. I lived in fear my entire life, and the religion I so faithfully practiced only fueled it each time I asked to hear the gospel and each time I sat down in that church pew.

It all makes sense to me now, looking back, why I so quickly ran out of the church as soon as the service was over, the fresh air bringing me reassurance that I would be okay. My conditioned brain was telling me I would be okay, but my body held the score.

CHAPTER NINE

My happy place. The place I would run to when flight took over me.

The ferns seemed to give off a new energy that day as I lay among them. The combination of yesterday's passing rainstorm and today's sunshine brought vibrance and life to everything it touched, and I couldn't help but drop my hands to the earth, feeling her vibrations flow through me. I felt calm, at peace, and safe. The ferns that surrounded the forest floor stood at about three feet tall, creating an entirely different perspective when sitting down.

The smell of dirt and life filled my nostrils, and I took a deep breath in. And with each breath, my heart stopped racing, and my mind became clear. I felt safe here among the tall evergreens that swayed above like that of a giant holding a baby, rocking back and forth slowly. The birds would sing their happy songs and I would get lost in their unpredictable melody and the variety of pitches they could reach. Deer would feed not too far away as the fawns ran about playing, and if the wind was in my favor, they wouldn't even notice me sitting there.

I would spend hours in this exact spot and time seemed to fade away. A monarch dragonfly would often buzz by, occasionally landing on a fern and locking eyes with me, but only for a brief, quick moment, then it was off again.

Anytime I was feeling anxious, nearly having a panic attack, I would run to the forest. I'd run to this spot, and there I would ground myself. This was how I (unknowingly) coped with the fact that my brother sexually abused me, or how I didn't feel safe in my own home. Of course, I didn't know this then—I was just trying to survive. I was constantly living in fight or flight, and in an instant, as soon as things got uncomfortable, I would run. Years down the road when I started seeing a counselor, she asked me if I ever was suicidal as a child, and I told her no. She informed me that most people who experience sexual trauma to the extent I did often weigh the option of continuing their life, but because I had such a profound connection to Mother Earth, that is what saved me.

As the three of us kids jumped off the school bus, Dixie, the bus driver, handed us a chocolate bar and told us to have a great summer and that she would see us in a few months.

Summer vacation was here, and excitement filled all of us, giving us an extra boost of energy to walk up the road to the house. *What adventures would we get into first?* I thought to myself as I trekked up the hill.

The smell of warm fresh cinnamon rolls filled the house and made my taste buds water as we walked through the carport door. Mom was always baking something, and today's choice was cinnamon rolls. It wouldn't take long before they would be gone, and she would need to bake something else. There were plenty of hungry bellies to feed, so Mom spent countless hours in the kitchen.

As I walked into the kitchen, Mom handed me a plate with a warm cinnamon roll covered with cream cheese frosting and I scarfed it down before running off to play. Tossing my licked-clean plate into the kitchen sink, I hollered, "Thanks for the cinnamon roll, Mom!" and ran into the living room where my sister was reading her book. "Want to go to the beaver pond and see if there are any ducks we can feed?" I asked.

"Yeah, let's do it! Mom, do we have any old bread that we can feed the ducks with?" my sister asked. Our mom replied that there indeed was some old bread in the corner of the cabinet, but to be careful not to take the potato bread she just bought for French toast for Sunday morning breakfast.

"We can swing on the tire swing too!" said my brother, who had decided to tag along.

We made our way across the field to an old gravel logging road that would take us up and over the hill to the beaver pond. The dark brown pond was halfway covered in lily pads that often had frogs on top of them, and the back half was surrounded by thick forest and an old clear-cut. Deer would occasionally come down to the water's edge to drink. Two small islands, covered in tall grasses and alder trees, sat in the middle of the pond and I always daydreamed of paddling out to them. The pond wasn't swimmable, but we spent hours alongside it fishing, catching frogs, and feeding the ducks that lived there.

"There they are!" I exclaimed as I pointed to the far side of the pond. The ducks had grown accustomed to us by now as they knew we always brought them food. Breaking the stale bread into small pieces, we threw them into the water. The ducks wasted no time, picking up the pieces one by one with their colorful beaks.

Running over to the big tire swing that hung from a giant maple tree, we took turns pushing each other. "Give me an underdog" was the famous term, and when doing so resulted in the tire spinning fast in circles, our hands tightly gripping the rope, causing us to giggle and throw back our heads, our blond hair falling behind us, glistening in the summer sun.

As the days got warmer and longer, our list of chores increased as well. Saturdays were always dedicated to deep cleaning the house—dusting, scrubbing toilets, mopping floors, cleaning our rooms, washing windows, and folding laundry. Every Saturday morning, Mom reminded us as we ate breakfast to bring down our pile of laundry so she could get started on it. As the loads finished, she would empty them in the living room creating several mounds of warm clean clothes. Sitting cross-legged, and often listening to an American cassette tape, we got to work folding. As I dusted the top of the piano, Mom instructed me to not forget to move things around and dust behind them. "Do it right first, otherwise you'll have to go back and do it again," Mom reminded me from the kitchen.

Photos of us kids and small decorations Mom had made sat on top of the old brown piano. My parents were always persistent about us doing our job right, whether we were loading the dishwasher or washing the windows. If it wasn't done right the first time, we would have to go back and do it again. Being lazy would get us nowhere, they always reminded us, and I'm thankful they taught us this mentality. As kids, it taught us from a young age to always take time and do it right, and when we got older, this would apply to many aspects of our lives.

Our house was three stories high, the two boys' bedrooms being in the basement, my parents on the main floor, and us girls slept in the two bedrooms upstairs. There were two living rooms, one having a wood fireplace that was always burning during the winter, with high vaulted ceilings and an elk and deer mount on the wall. This was the room where we celebrated Christmas, and typically, when company was over, this was the room the parents visited in. Many times, when we had company, we kids would surround the piano and sing from the "Songs and Hymns of Zion" booklet as my sister played. There was no lack of talent, and I believe if any of us went on to be professional singers, we would have made a very successful career in doing so. Singing was encouraged as a child of God, and there, shoulder to shoulder, we stood around the piano, our parents listening to our angelic voices.

As summer continued, the bottoms of our feet went from soft to calloused, our hair turned bleached white, and our skin went from white to dark brown highlighted with freckles, as the entirety of most days were spent under the sun.

One afternoon when my parents had to run to town to buy some gardening supplies, we got bored and wished we had a swimming pool to cool off in.

"I've got an idea. Go grab a couple shovels and a tarp!" my older brother instructed us.

I find our actions hilarious as this would never fly with Mom and Dad, but we did it anyway. Using the shovels, we started to dig a hole in the middle of the field. We were going to make a swimming hole! The hole was roughly a foot deep by eight feet wide when we decided that was deep enough to cool off in. Throwing the tarp into the dirt, we grabbed the garden hose attached to the shop and started to fill it up.

For the next couple of hours, our imaginations went wild as we played crocodiles and zebras in a water hole in Africa. One of us was the crocodile, lying flat in the water, our nose blowing bubbles on the dark surface while we would sneak up on our sibling playing the zebra on the water's edge. As we splashed about, the water quickly turned muddy, the tarp clearly not doing much good to keep the mud out. Hearing someone holler at us, our imaginations quickly got shut down as Dad came storming across the field.

"What do you think you're doing? Empty that now and fill it back up with dirt!" Dad insisted. The rest of the afternoon consisted of cleaning up the water hole, yet we couldn't help but chuckle as we did so.

CHAPTER TEN

Every summer in August, we would take a family trip to a campground called Takhlakh Lake, located at the base of Mt. Adams. This was always the highlight of my summer, and every summer break I eagerly waited till we would head toward the mountain.

"I'm headed to the store to buy the groceries we need for this camping trip. While I'm gone, I want all of you to pack your bags. Don't forget your toothbrush, swimsuits, and sleeping bags," Mom instructed us as she grabbed her purse from the top of the fridge.

"Mom! Can you please buy me a one-time-use disposable camera?" I begged. Photography was my newfound hobby and luckily my mom supported it and would buy me a camera most times I asked for it.

"Sure, but please pack while I am gone."

That wasn't going to be an issue as I was already packed and ready to go. The rest of the day was like watching paint dry, as we weren't leaving till the next morning. Finally, morning came, and after a breakfast of sugary cold cereal, we packed up the van, attached the camper to Dad's truck, and hit the road.

We always camped with our cousins and would meet the families at a small grocery store in Randle, Washington. The last chance to use a real bathroom or grab necessities before leaving society behind, hitting the windy, gravel road to the campground.

Upon arriving, we set up our tents before going off to play, while Dad set up the camper and Mom got the kitchen organized.

"Who wants to go swimming?" one of the siblings hollered, and in response, we all said, "Me!"

"We have to blow up the raft and tubes first," my older sister reminded us.

Towels, tubes, and raft in hand, we used the trail to get to the lake. The view was breathtaking. Surrounding the glistening lake were tall fir trees with lime-green, mossy branches. Sandy beaches were scattered along the shoreline, and small colorful canoes floated on the lake as other campers fished for trout. Nestled behind the lake was the beautiful Mt. Adams, still covered in snow. Flies and birds hovered above the lake, and the fish would jump about creating small circular ripples on the calm surface of the water.

Our playful voices from the lake would echo across and into the campground as we played for hours among the water. The high-country lake was chilly, but as we played king of the raft or paddled around in the tubes, we distracted ourselves from the cold water.

One afternoon, a few of us girls took out the raft to the middle of the lake. Wanting to be done, I decided to jump out and swim back to shore. I didn't factor in that we had been swimming for hours now and didn't realize how tired my body was until I started swimming back. The wind was in my face, creating white caps that splashed in my eyes and mouth, making it difficult to see and breathe. My breaths became heavy, and my heart rate increased as I screamed for help. I turned on my back to try and conserve my energy but with every kick, I felt like I wasn't making progress. It didn't take long before my aunt swam out to help get me back to shore.

The following five days were spent fishing, biking, swimming, hiking up to the base of the mountain, roasting marshmallows over the fire, telling stories by the fire, night games—the list goes on.

The energy of twenty-plus kids running around was buzzing throughout the campground, and there was always someone to play with. I preferred to sleep under the stars, as others did too, and after a long day of play, we would lay on our backs counting shooting stars and giggling about certain events of the day.

The first day of camping was over, and I had already used up my entire film camera, as I snapped photos of the lake and the kids playing.

The next day, a group of us hiked to the base of the mountain. The trailhead would take us four miles one way, passing through dark timber, along meadows of colorful flowers, and across various small streams. The moms always held up the back of the pact as the kids took charge ahead. There was something so special about being in a place where only so many humans have stepped foot before.

There was a feeling of wild energy and peacefulness that came over you while hiking. Often, I would slow or speed up my pace, wanting to be alone while I hiked. I was in search of connection, and while I hiked alone in the quiet, my mind would slow down as I enjoyed the scenery around me and the physical effort it took to move up the mountain.

As we approached the boulder field, it was covered in several feet of snow still. With nearly every step, we post-holed to our knees, and snowball fights broke out. Reaching the end point, we enjoyed a chicken sandwich Mom had made and a sweet treat of some sort before heading back down. Sliding on our butts, we slipped and slid down the snow, and then raced down the trail to try and be the first one back to the van. The days seemed to fly by, and I dreaded having to go home.

On the last night at camp, my dad, uncle, and brothers built a sauna next to the lake. One of my uncles brought his portable stove in, which we piled rocks on top and built a fire below. We let the fire burn until the rocks were nice and hot, and then it was time to sauna and swim. There were roughly ten blonde kids crammed inside the sauna at once, the steam filling it up and burning our faces.

"Who's ready to swim?" someone inevitably asked, and one

by one we exited the tarp, running and jumping into the lake to cool off.

Laying on my back in the water, I looked up at the starry night sky in all its glory. Meteors would often flash by as our voices echoed across the lake, surely entertaining our fellow campers. The water soon cooled us off and, trying not to trip on the shoreline, we ran back into the sauna for another round. The warm steamy air was welcoming as we filled in one after another.

In this moment, nothing else mattered, as we were consumed in pure joy. These moments will forever be ingrained in my memory, and looking around at the smiling faces, I soaked up every minute of it. I wanted to live in this moment forever, where everyone was full of love and happy energy.

"Who's ready to jump in?" one of my cousins asked.

"Let's go!" everyone responded at once, and so the night went on. Returning to camp, our hair wet, we bundled up and sat around the campfire roasting marshmallows, and with sticky fingers, we ate to our hearts' desire.

CHAPTER ELEVEN

Summer was nearly over, and it was time to preserve the vegetables from the garden. This was an all-hands-on-deck task.

Starting in the garden, we were to pick all the remaining corn and husk it. Our horse, Tinker, was happy as we pulled back the husk and tossed it over the fence to him. After finishing husking the corn, we brought it inside and got set up for the next process.

First, we would rinse the corn, then boil it. After the corn was cooked, it would get shuffled to the kitchen table where two of us would use the corn on the cob stripper, creating small piles of corn. Mom would then fill small square containers and toss them into the freezer.

Next up was green beans: After picking the beans, we would rinse and then snap them in half, once again making piles all over the kitchen table so it was easy for Mom to grab them and toss them into the pressure cooker. We would also make dill pickles from our cucumbers, freeze the zucchini, and pickle the beets. These vegetables would help feed us throughout the winter, and we made sure none of it went to waste.

The apples from the trees would get pilled, cut up, and cooked, then smashed into applesauce. The raspberries, strawberries, and blackberries would get made into homemade jam and several bags would get set aside for homemade pie. Living off the land was a full-time job, but with the many hands, it typically made for quick and easy work. There was a deep connection to most of our food growing up, and we savored every bite.

Most of my memories from growing up are that of hunting,

outdoor adventures, the repetitive Sunday and Wednesday church services, and the holidays. The in-between seems to be slightly foggy, especially as I reached my teen years.

After my abuse, I went into a flight-or-fight mode, where I went through the mundane motions every day, walking through a fog. I used my bubbly personality to get through most social events and spent most of my time alone wandering the forest with my mom's camera. I had completely suppressed the memory of my brother raping and molesting me and often questioned if I was depressed. *There's no way you could be depressed*, I told myself as I played back many times how I entertained a room full of people.

The practice of the LLC detours believers from dealing with issues at hand, for when feelings are hurt, or something upsetting happens, it's brushed under the rug, the gospel's power brainwashing you to forget it. This caused a lack of communication and processing of emotions in the family. Overall, there was a lack of discussion (unless it was related to particular sins) growing up, and many years later, when I left the LLC, I realized how much work it took to have a healthy relationship with someone without running away from my feelings.

I knew my parents loved me, but with fourteen children, I could see it was difficult for them to show love and affection toward us all individually. Some nights I would walk into the kitchen seeing Mom standing at the stove, keeping herself busy as she stirred dinner. I could see the emotion on her face as she held back tears.

"What's wrong, Mom?" I would ask her. Dropping the wooden spoon on the counter, pasta sauce splattering all over the counter and floor, she would run off to the bedroom, bursting into tears. Most times I would give her a few minutes and then wander into the room to give her a big hug.

"I just can't seem to do anything right and ... I'm just *so tired* ..." Mom once told me as she cried and wiped her eyes, trying to be strong in front of her little girl. I wanted to squeeze all the sadness out of her as I could see she was clearly exhausted. I can't blame my parents for the lack of affection, nor do I think they were intentionally doing so, for I can't imagine having fourteen children and being capable of doing so. Mom's job was to take care of the house, raise her children, and proceed to have babies as God willed it; and Dad's purpose in life was to support the family.

We spent many evenings and weekends with our cousins. We would spend hours outside playing night games such as kick the can, cops and robbers, and ditch. We knew when it was time to come in—when the back porch light flicked on and off. Yet despite the many hours we spent together, I never had a deep, emotional, open, and authentic relationship with anyone as conversations never got too deep or serious. I never felt comfortable being able to talk to my sisters or friends about things that were bothering me, and they never came to me either.

Despite the lack of affection from my parents, I took every opportunity I could to connect with them. My dad and I would watch hunting films while I massaged his feet. To this day he claims I was the one who cured the back pain he suffered from his job. Anytime Dad was going fishing or hunting, I would always tag along. With my mom, I would hang out with her as she baked cakes, cookies, and bread. Bit by bit, she would teach me, and eventually, I was in the kitchen baking things on my own.

I always felt this need to stay busy, I always needed to be moving, otherwise, I would go crazy, often running to the forest or the pond to calm down. I'm sure if my parents brought me to the doctor, I would have been diagnosed with ADHD and then put on medication.

The older I got, the more disconnected I started to feel with the church and the people who attended it, but I forced myself to push the thoughts and feelings aside. This was the only true religion to practice, and if I didn't do so, I would burn forever in the eternity of hell. Or that's what they preached to us anyway.

Most of my early teenage years are completely erased from

my memory and I can't help but wonder about those few years and the things I experienced. I was a lost soul, hiding behind baggy clothes. I always pulled my hair back tight, ready to fight if I needed to. From the photos I see of myself from those years, I see pain and fear in my eyes. My tomboy appearance would surely keep the perpetrators away, for who wants to go after a girl that looks like a boy? I walked around as if I was going into battle, my stance strong and abrasive. Many years later, a guy friend would ask me, "Draya, why are you always punching people?" This was my reaction when I would be teased by guys: One time, my brother started wrestling me and I knocked a few of his ribs out of place, or another time when a raft guide jokingly put me in a headlock, I hit his balls so hard he fell to the ground and could barely breathe; and another time, I dumped a cup full of water onto a friend's bed when having a bad trip on mushrooms.

I didn't trust men, and anytime I was triggered, I did anything I could to prove they didn't want to mess with me. My body held the score as I carried my trauma with me everywhere I went, trusting nobody and constantly watching my back.

CHAPTER TWELVE

At ages fourteen and fifteen, we attended a confirmation camp in the summer. By attending, completing, and then confirming with the holy communion, we then became a "young kid." Attending camps, discussions, and gatherings of the young encouraged us to further continue our work as a child of God after we were confirmed. I like to call this event "adult baptism." This camp was roughly eight days long, the class was that of roughly forty students, a handful of bigs, directors, ministers, teachers, camp counselors, a camp caretaker, and a camp manager.

I talked previously in the book about attending youth camps as a child—well, confirmation camp was like that, only way more intense. Upon arriving at camp, each student was handed a booklet that had each day's lessons, sections for your goals and hopes as a child of God, verses from hymns and quotes from the Bible, questions we were to answer, and a section to take notes. These lessons covered topics such as *"God, our Heavenly Father: God is our creator, God hates sin but loves the sinner,"* and the following questions were assigned to this lesson: *"What is the most important matter in your life?* **To be a believer, living faith, getting to heaven, and having your sins forgiven."* Question number two: *"How has God created the visible and invisible world?* **By his word.**" Another example of the lessons we so seriously studied is *"Music, 'Sing O People of the Lord.' Objective: Music is a gift from God, and a tool of the enemy of souls; Wholesome music helps to fight against temptation and sin."*

Some of the questions in the booklet were that of:

- Explain what the core of the gospel is and why it is important to me, a believer.
- Explain the difference between sin and temptation and give examples of each.
- Explain how God established marriage for the benefit of mankind.
- Describe what the conscience is and how it functions.
- Compare and contrast temporal, spiritual and eternal death and give examples of each.
- Explain how sexuality is a gift from God.
- What is the mother of all sins? **Unbelief**.

These are just a few examples of our studies at camp. These lessons were to be taken very seriously, for as we got older, more temptations would arise (sex, music, movies), and within a few years, we would graduate high school and leave the nest our parents had built us. It was time to lay down the whip on us and deliver as much Bible talk and brainwashing as possible.

Each day was filled with hours studying these lessons and preparing for our confirmation examination at the end of camp. This examination consisted of a variety of questions. Here are a few examples followed by the answers:

- What is the most important matter in your life? **To be a believer. Living faith, getting to heaven, having my sins forgiven.**
- What is sin? **Sin is thoughts, words, and deeds that are contrary to God's will.**
- To whom does the Law belong according to the Bible? **To the unbelieving.**
- Who is an acceptable communion guest? **A believer.**

Following these intense questions, we had to recite the baptismal command, the Lord's Prayer, and the benediction. When we had passed the written exam, it was time to receive the holy communion at the pulpit, in front of our family and friends. We had put in the time, we studied hard, and now we must decide to accept this meal of remembrance.

The day for our first holy communion was upon us as we put on our white dresses and curled our hair.

"Are you nervous?" everyone asked each other, knowing in just a short time we would be standing in front of hundreds of people accepting our first communion. The church was packed full, some people even having to stand in the back. We found our placement and formed the lines in which we would walk up toward the front, in front of the many fellow believers.

The organ started to play our song and we got instructions to walk up. All eyes were on us now; this was a big day for a child of God. The service began with an opening hymn followed by a sermon, the minister delivering a message on the importance of this time as a young child of God, and the receiving of the first communion, a meal of remembrance.

Objective: Communion is a meal of remembrance that strengthens the faith of a child of God. When in faith, we receive the bread and the wine (grape juice), we receive the body and blood of Christ.

As one row was called at a time, we stood in a line in front of the several ministers with trays in their hands. The faces of these men were stern and serious as they avoided eye contact with us. First, we received a wafer, "the bread of life," and as we received this wafer, we would raise our right hand and the minister would respond with the gospel, forgiving all our sins and renewing the Holy Spirit within us. Following the wafer and gospel was the grape juice, "the blood of Christ."

Looking down the line of students, I saw tears rolling down some faces, and some of them even exchanged hugs, sobbing into each other's shoulders. This was real, this was working. Everything we'd been taught throughout our life and at camp—it all fell on our shoulders at this moment. We were children of God, and we now knew our mission in life. Of course, during this time, I was oblivious to the perspective I have now. I was just another child of God going through the motions. After eight days of studying and lessons, I felt that if I had died at that moment, I was acceptable to heaven.

As I looked out at the crowd watching, I saw my parents in a pew. My dad's arm was around my mom's shoulder as they, too, wiped the tears falling from their eyes. The church was exploding in sobs as students left the pulpit and went to their parents to hug them, and so I did as well. My parents welcomed me with open arms as I walked up to them, praising me on my first confirmation and for graduating. They told me how proud they were of me and that they loved me so much. I could feel their love and support more than I ever had in life.

As the day went on, more hugs were given to me as we mingled outside the church. We took family photos of this special and important day in my life as a child of God. I was the eleventh child of my parents to complete confirmation camp and accept the holy communion, and I could see the pride in their faces as they were reassured that their work raising me was done correctly.

CHAPTER THIRTEEN

Packing our hunting gear into Dad's truck, we took off toward Klickitat, Washington, a small town along the massive Columbia River, a couple hours east of our house. This was an annual hunting trip that we kids would take with Dad and was a highlight of our year.

Anticipation filled our imaginations as we made the drive across the river, getting closer to our destination. The windy road brought us to a free campground next to the river, where we set up camp and enjoyed hotdogs over the fire. As the evening went on, the campground became more packed with other hunters pulling in with their campers and trailers.

The question always lay under the surface if we would see anyone in our secret spot on the next morning's hunt. Dad made sure we were up earlier than anyone else so that wouldn't be the case. We enjoyed the warmth of the crackling fire and got our packs ready for the next day's hunt. Settling into my sleeping bag for the night, I listened to the hum of the creek and the muffled conversations from the other hunters in camp. Sleep never came that night, as my imagination of tomorrow's hunt kept me awake. Soon the alarm sounded, and it was time to lace up the boots and start the trek up the steep hill.

When I say steep, I mean *steep*. The grass and acorns often made us slip as we dredged up the mountain. We learned quickly to dress light, as our sweat would soak through all our clothes before we were halfway up the hill. Our hunting clothes were baggy and hot—Mom sewed unisex pants, shirts, and hoodies made from fleece or cotton. With each step, our legs burned, and our lungs screamed for more oxygen. Leading the way, Dad would stop every hundred yards for a break, and our hearts would pound in our chests as we looked up and enjoyed the stars twinkling above us. I always thought it was so cool that I was on some mountainside looking at the stars with sweat dripping off my face while most people were still sleeping.

Reaching the top always brought a breath of relief, knowing the hardest part was done. With limited darkness left, we all spread out between two drainages so we could cover as much ground as possible. Headlamps would fade off into the distance as my siblings headed to their spots.

Turning on my radio and putting on an extra layer due to my sweaty chill, I watched the sunrise as it turned the sky bright orange. I loaded my rifle, knowing what was about to go down: The deer would feed on the agricultural fields at night and come early morning they would make their way to the pines to bed down for the day, and in doing so, they would cross right past us.

Pulling up my binoculars, I saw several does on the far horizon line, with a buck following them. I called out on the radio letting everyone know I had deer spotted and to get ready. More and more deer appeared on the horizon and my heart started to beat faster in my chest. Soon sounds of rifles firing echoed through and across the valley below.

On this hunt, I was covering a route where the deer used a game trail as they headed to their bedding grounds. The trail went along the side of the hill, clearly used by generations of deer. Seeing a small buck and several does head my way, I settled my .270 on the branch in front of me and waited for a broadside shot. Making a grunt noise with my mouth, the deer stopped, I took aim, and slowly pulled the trigger.

I radioed my dad and let him know I had just shot a buck. I could hear the excitement in his voice, and he reassured me that he and my siblings would make their way to me. Soon I saw my dad and siblings come over the skyline of the hillside with big smiles on their faces! We all exchanged high-fives and hugs as they walked toward me.

Starting where the buck had stood, we followed the blood trail and, soon enough, saw him piled up not too far off. A clean double-lung shot. This buck hadn't suffered, and no meat was ruined. All hands worked together as Dad cut the hide away. Someone held the leg, and others transferred the meat to game bags. I intently watched Dad as I held onto the buck's hindquarter, memorizing each slice of his knife, impressed by his quick and smooth work.

CHAPTER FOURTEEN

Sitting at my desk during high school, I avoided eye contact with those around me, and when we had free time in class, I sat there alone at my desk, keeping my eyes down. I lacked the skills to engage with classmates who were not believers. We didn't have anything in common so what would we talk about? Bullying from certain schoolmates would occur as they made incest jokes toward us and always made comments on how there were so many of us.

One afternoon, my cousin was crying at lunch, and I asked her what was wrong. She told me how these boys kept teasing her and making jokes about how we are different. I had enough of this bullying, and without hesitation, I walked up to the group of four guys standing in a circle.

Standing at just five feet tall, I shoved the leader of the group into the vending machine. A look of surprise came over all their faces and they went silent. I still had him pushed up against the vending machine when I pointed my finger in his face, spit flying out of my angry mouth as I told him, "You have no right to treat us the way you do. You better stop, and if you don't, you better watch your back."

"I'm so sorry, it won't happen again," he reassured me through his weak and scared voice. Standing tall and puffing out my chest, I walked away without another word. From that day forward, the bullying stopped from this group of guys, and over the next couple of years, they became friendly classmates.

Not being able to participate in school sports was an ingredient to my low self-esteem growing up. Coaches nearly begged us to participate in sports as they saw our natural talent, but we always had to politely decline due to our religious beliefs. I was and still am a competitive person, and as a teenager, I dreamed of running out on the field, making goals, or diving and saving a volleyball from hitting the ground. But participating in sports was too much of a temptation and could lead to a life of self-glory and a competitive addiction that could steer us away from the church. How would a child of God be able to raise a Christian family while out traveling, competing at a high level of sport?

That's just the thing, many of us would have succeeded in the sports world due to our Scandinavian genetics. I know this firsthand as many afternoons and late nights were spent playing volleyball. Located in the back of the church's parking lot was a volleyball court and as day turned to night, the bright automatic light shone over us as we played game after game. The guys would play hockey every Saturday night and we girls would always go and cheer them on. I even suited up in full gear a few times and joined them. I'm sure it was a comical sight to see as we girls tried to keep the puck away from the guys.

I graced through high school with good grades, an average GPA of 3.6. To be honest, I didn't try that hard because I knew, as a woman in the LLC, I would most likely get married out of high school and wouldn't attend college. I knew I loved photography but didn't seem to have a passion for anything worth studying.

I felt like I had no direction or even a choice in my future. The ministers and my parents would tell me all I needed to do was trust that it was all in God's hands. I found connections with a few teachers— the football coach, the photography teacher, and the PE teacher. I helped in the gym as a teacher's assistant and took four years of photography, so I got to know these teachers well. I also babysat their girls when they would go out for date nights. The girls and I would devour pizza, popcorn, and ice cream while we watched movies. After the girls went to bed, I sat glued in front of the TV, my dopamine levels through the roof. I was starting to get a glimpse of what the world looked like outside of the LLC and I often daydreamed of leaving it and exploring the wonders of the world. The thought would come and go, for I knew if I was living under my parents' roof there was no way I could leave the LLC. I told myself, *Someday when I'm older, I'll do it.*

I can't remember my exact age, but it was a summer during my high school years when my brother and his wife had their first babies—twin girls. This story here proves how disconnected I was from the fact that this brother sexually abused and molested me.

My sister-in-law had to have a C-section with her twins, and for some reason, I volunteered to go to Colorado for a couple of weeks and help them with the babies and household chores. It breaks my heart to think back to that version of myself. How could I have forgotten about such a horrific event? How could I even stand being around my brother? It boggles my mind to think these things were possible. The pressure to believe that my sins were forgiven, forgotten, and washed away in the sea of grace forever really messed with me growing up.

I have heard countless stories of others from the LLC about being abused as well and suffering from the same suppression of the memory due to the requirement to have your sins forgiven, so that you were heaven-acceptable. This teaching has bred narcissists, rapists, molesters, along with emotional and verbal abusers.

I was so blinded by this, but as soon as I left the religion behind, it became crystal clear how pertinent the issue was. Personally, I know of fifteen-plus people who have suffered some type of abuse, and it was all hidden behind the Holy Bible. I'm not trying to say this is the only religion that abuse happens in but when living a life of narrow-mindedness, fear of not being heaven-acceptable, being sheltered from the world—the real world, where bad things are talked about—it becomes a breeding ground for unacceptable behavior.

I had a cousin who molested his own nieces at (roughly) age

sixteen. His father was a narcissist who cheated on his wife and treated his kids like they were dirt. A generational issue passed down all because the use of the gospel was just so damn easy to take advantage of.

Another one of my cousins was molested by her cousin, and the cousin that molested her was molested by her father. It's a trend that needs to stop which can only happen if we continue to talk about, and to own our story.

CHAPTER FIFTEEN

As I approached the end of my last year of high school, I had no plans of attending college and, frankly, no idea what I wanted to do with my life. I didn't stress about it much as most ladies in the LLC typically got married within a couple of years after graduating high school. I figured that's what would happen with me.

My sister, cousin, and I decided to move into a house together and I was more than ready to get out of my parents' home, to be independent, and to have my own space. I was working at a nursing home at the time, bouncing around in the kitchen cooking, serving food, or cleaning.

I was able to watch movies and listen to music freely now that I wasn't living with my parents. My sister and cousin participated in this as well, so there was nothing to hide. We would spend an entire lazy Saturday watching movies, then go to church on Sunday and have our sins forgiven. We were such rebels, or that's what we rebels perceived as. Watching movies and listening to music was a sin, but we freely walked the line of temptation.

It didn't take long until I met my first love. We both fell headfirst into this relationship. He was ten years older than me, a nurse from Arizona, and had his own place. Such great qualities in a future husband, my friends told me. I was giddy and so in love. I had been fighting for attention my entire life, and here and now I was validated through this new and exciting relationship.

He came out to Washington to meet my family and fit right in. We couldn't keep our hands off each other and I dreamed about marrying this man and starting a family. I was consumed by the idea of love.

We had been dating for roughly six months when we decided to meet in Colorado for my cousin's wedding. During the week leading up to my trip, he became very distant. I tried calling him several times and he would never pick up. My gut didn't like this, and I dreaded my trip to Colorado.

Upon arriving, we wasted no time getting alone so we could talk. He informed me that he couldn't picture himself marrying me and that, ultimately, he needed to end the relationship. I was completely crushed. Suddenly, my future seemed dark and dull, and self-doubt consumed me. I felt as though I wasn't good enough, not pretty enough, skinny enough, and undeserving of love. I couldn't even think about him and his reasons for ending the relationship, for I was so consumed by my mind and all the negative talk that was happening.

Eventually, like all heartbreak, I moved on and something inside me shifted. I became more aware of my emotions and of love, which in return made those traumatic memories surface in the quiet moments I was alone. Having my heart broken was one of the best things that could have happened to me. As they say, you must go through the dark before you reach the light. The darkness was coming, and my depressive state of mind welcomed it with open arms.

My sister, a couple of cousins, and I moved into a house, and I was looking forward to a new chapter. It was time to heal my heartbreak. The house was old and broken down, but with three bedrooms, hardwood floors, and a big, open living room with a wood stove, we loved it! We had a giant backyard and a covered patio in the back. We set up a volleyball net and would have friends over almost every weekend. It was the girls' pad and there was always something going on.

Living with these girls there was still a lack of connection as conversations never seemed to go deeper than the surface area. I felt alone despite the buzzing house, and then things started to get weird.

I started experiencing a lot of anxiety, couldn't sleep at night, and I would get these crazy emotional mood swings where I went from happy to crying my eyes out within minutes. I didn't tell anyone about these episodes because I was too ashamed. I had become the ultimate expert at masking my feelings, but for some reason, things started to change, and I could no longer control them. I asked myself over and over, *Am I depressed? Bipolar? Nah, you're good*, I would tell myself, *Look how happy you are; you laugh all the time.*

I missed having the forest behind the house I could escape to. Many times, I would get in my car and drive there. I played sad country songs on repeat and became consumed by them. My sister once asked me why I was always listening to sad songs. I knew I needed help; I knew I needed something to change, but I didn't know what that was quite yet.

One fall afternoon, my parents' yellow lab Daisy got unexpectedly pregnant from our cousin's black lab, and she was soon due to deliver them. I daydreamed of keeping one but didn't think I could take on the work that comes with raising a good dog. Soon, Daisy had her puppies, nine beautiful white, black, and yellow labs. The last one born, also known as the "runt," was the weakest, and physically, it struggled to get food fast enough and keep up with its quickly growing siblings. It broke my heart to see this pup fight so hard to live. I saw my opportunity and told my parents I wanted to keep this puppy, and that I would make sure she was warm and would help feed her.

So, I did, and she slowly began to get stronger and bigger, but suddenly, she got sick. I couldn't let this pup die, for she had been fighting so hard ever since she was born, and I wasn't going to let it happen.

"I'll bring her to the vet, and I'll pay for it. She's mine now. I'll name her Adina," I told my parents, as I snuggled her to my chest. It felt so good to have something to take care of and to love something so much. I dropped her off at the vet, and they told me they would call me when they had news.

The phone rang not long after I got home and the vet informed me Adina had Parvo, a sickness that would cause severe disease and most likely kill her if she wasn't given treatment, so I gave them the go-ahead to treat her. I knew she was in good hands; it was just a matter of time before I got her back. I was so happy to receive the call that Adina was well, and it was time to bring her home. She was so happy to be back with me and to be able to sleep on my pillow at night. She was small and weak but had endless energy, and soon she was back to being a healthy puppy.

Having Adina got me out of bed in the morning and out of the house during the day. She was a very sweet pup, and her tail was always wagging back and forth. Adina and I would venture out on adventures to the river or through the forest behind my parents' house. We did everything together; we were best friends. But despite her unconditional love, I couldn't escape my demons, and I would break out in deep heavy sobs. Her tail wagging, Adina would lay next to me, resting her head on my legs, her big eyes looking up at me. She would give me kisses and stay next to me until I decided it was time to get up.

She was my lifeline; she was my rock.

PART TWO

CHAPTER SIXTEEN

Upon returning home from a trip to Colorado, the rainy Washington weather made it hard to cope with my underlying depression, so I decided to look for jobs in Colorado. I applied for multiple postings on a website where families look for nannies. My phone rang and looking down, I saw a message from Phoebe Larsson.

"Can you be here Monday for an interview at the Blue Bird Cafe, let's say ten a.m.?"

"Yes," I responded. I was moving to Colorado! I needed to find a new home for Adina for I didn't have room in my car nor did my living arrangement allow it. I reached out to a friend I grew up with. She was newly married, and she and her husband lived on a farm just on the other side of the river. They already had a dog, and I thought this would make a great home for Adina. They thought about it and agreed they would love to take her on. They came to my parents' house to pick her up, and I knew Adina had served her time with me and it was time to let her go.

As I rubbed her soft ears and kissed her nose one last time, we looked into each other's eyes, so grateful for the adventures and love we shared together. I made temporary living arrangements with my brother and his wife, packed up my car, and headed toward the Rocky Mountains. As I buckled my seatbelt, it was almost as though I was bracing for what was ahead. Whatever it was, I was ready.

Moving to Colorado set my life into motion. The process of awakening to my abuse and all that was trapped within me was about to unfold. I could sense the change but didn't know what it was, like distant movement on the far horizon. I was curious, and I wanted to get closer. But that journey would take time, and it would be very, very difficult, resembling that of the Oregon Trail—each day a battle on its own and unknown to the next. The challenges ahead would hit me like a tidal wave, throwing my body into the ocean floor and unleashing its merciless wrath. Soon, intense and life-changing events would occur and I'm sure they will continue to do so as I grow older. That's just the thing, life will constantly test you, but it's up to you to decide whether to show up. The smallest change in our habits can set the ball rolling downhill, picking up speed as it goes, becoming an unstoppable force to be reckoned with.

During my first couple of years in Colorado, I moved around a lot, living with various girls from the church, from one place to the next. Living in a new environment caused an uneasiness that I knew exactly how to forget. I entertained, I made people laugh, and many times, I was the center of attention at any gathering, standing in front of nearly a hundred people, acting like a goof. In return, my memories of sadness and self-pity would disappear, along with my overall lack of feeling. I was in full survivor mode. Nobody ever talked about hard things when the room was full of laughter, and I took the bait and ran with it.

One evening as I was sitting on a couch at haps, a term used for the gathering of the young LLC adults, someone told me to jump up and start "Foolish." Foolish was a game where one person had to stand in the middle of the room and act funny. Whoever laughed first was up next! I had a knack for this, and people would insist on me starting the game. But when asked on one particular evening, I had no desire to anymore. I was tired of putting on a show, hiding the real me deep within my sorrow. I felt like a fake who was lost among a group of people who would often judge others and hide their real feelings behind the phrase, Holy Spirit. I didn't understand why I struggled to connect with others and started to feel depressed and lonely.

I found a deep friendship with Trevor, who was also in the LLC. His energy was different, and I felt a connection with him, unlike many within the LLC. We shared a common love for wild places and would fill our time together rafting a river or hiking up some mountain. Good conversations naturally occurred and were filled with depth and tales of adventure. A like-minded soul that challenged me to harness my confidence and to follow my heart. I felt free to speak my truth in his presence, and later down the road, when I hit rock bottom during the early morning hours, he was the one I wanted to speak to.

CHAPTER SEVENTEEN

It was wintertime and I was headed to Minnesota to photograph a good friend's wedding. I was excited to get out of town and see friends I didn't get to see very often.

I was walking through the lobby when I caught the eye of one of the groomsmen. He was tall, blond, and handsome. My heart skipped a beat as we locked eyes across the lobby. In the busyness of the day, we didn't have a chance to connect alone, but within a few weeks, we were chatting on the phone for hours, planning to see each other soon.

Life suddenly was all about this man whom I thought I loved. We started long-distance dating, and over the next few months, we met each other's families and continued to spend endless hours talking over the phone. It didn't take long before we started talking about marriage and where we would live. Montana was the deciding factor, for I couldn't bring myself to live in a state without mountains, and the mountains of Colorado made him claustrophobic. So, we decided on Montana, plus we had friends that lived there too!

I felt like I was living in a dream, an LLC dream. I even messaged Phoebe Larsson saying I might not return the next year because I was going to get married and move to Montana. I was sure of it.

After dating for a while, Lance came out to Colorado to surprise me. I was at a family gathering playing outside with some nieces and nephews when a man with dark skin and a cowboy hat came walking up the driveway, hollering at me, asking for directions. I was thrown off for a second but quickly realized it was Geoff under the disguise. My oldest brother helped plan the surprise and was excited to see it play out. I felt overwhelmed with love, but guilt instantly crept in and found itself in my heart.

I remember this moment so vividly. This moment changed my life. As Geoff and I hugged in the driveway of my brother's house, my life flashed before my eyes. I was nineteen at the time. What would life look like if we did get married? I saw my future self: I was pregnant, standing in our living room, a dirty diaper in my hand. There were two kids, one was playing about and the other one was crying, screaming about something. The house was a mess, empty milk bottles and dirty diapers littered the floor; my hair was a mess, I was overweight, sleepy-eyed, and exhausted. I felt like a horrible mom, wife, and human. I was depressed, lonely, suicidal, and felt no sexual desire for the man I laid next to at night.

This was not the life I had envisioned as a young girl when I daydreamed about marriage. Then, the selfish part of my brain kicked in, and thoughts circled about not being able to hunt for a long while so I could tend to my children, house, and husband. Not believing in birth control, I knew the children would keep coming until my body was too old to reproduce anymore.

And then the question hit me like a ton of bricks: *How can I fully love this man, marry him, and raise a family with him if I don't even love myself? And most importantly, how can I marry a man who I can't tell my deepest darkest secret to?* I knew marrying Geoff wasn't the answer, and I knew at that moment I didn't love him the way you should love a person you plan to marry. I didn't even love myself. I had some work to do, and I knew I had to break this man's heart.

The chatter and laughter from the porch brought me out of this trance. I had to get my act together; I had to do what I was so good at: pretending everything was okay. Giving Lance another big hug, we made our way into the house to visit with the adults.

Let me take you back a couple of years to my brother's wedding in Minnesota. A few of my sisters, sisters-in-law, and myself were driving down the interstate when someone said, "Did you girls hear what happened to Autumn?" I had never been one for gossip, unlike most ladies in the church who seem to thrive off it. Not paying much attention to the gossip, I continued to look out the window watching the corn fields go by, lost in thought.

"Turns out she was molested by her dad, and now he is in jail!" one of the girls said. My head, which was resting on the window, shot up, like a natural reflex to a hammer hitting your knee at the doctor. My heart sank, my stomach twisted and turned, a hot flash went through my body, and I felt like I was going to throw up.

After ten years of suppression, the sexual abuse I suffered from my brother flashed before my eyes. I felt so bad for Autumn, but at the same time, I realized the depth of what happened to me. We were headed to a family function and my brother would be there. *Now was not the time to be dealing with this,* I told myself. *You must push it aside and deal with it later, you can do this,* I thought over and over. *You must forget about your abuse, you must be strong. God forgave these sins long ago, remember?* I don't remember the rest of that car ride nor do I remember much from that trip in general. What I did know was I had a secret that was trying to surface, and I didn't want anything to do with it.

My new boyfriend stayed in town after the surprise, and he could sense I was acting different and distant. He asked me what was up, and I asked him to go for a walk. I knew what I had to do, and I felt sick knowing I was prolonging the situation.

Using some excuse that I can't remember, I ended the relationship. I wanted to tell him that I needed help; I wanted to tell him I was sexually abused when I was a young girl. I wanted to tell him that I'd been keeping it a secret for my entire life, that I didn't love myself, and that I needed to see a counselor because I was all sorts of fucked up. I wanted to tell him that I needed to find love within myself before I could give it to anyone else, let alone start raising a family.

I didn't tell him any of these things because of the fear that was bred inside me ever since I was old enough to comprehend the teachings of the LLC. I wanted to show him compassion as he wept in my arms, but honestly, I didn't have any to give. I was completely overwhelmed by the fact that I needed to confront this suppressed memory that kept surfacing. I was overloaded with emotions such as anger, frustration, and confusion.

CHAPTER EIGHTEEN

A few nights later I was at another church gathering when my good friend, Amy, asked me if I had ever thought about joining a weight-lifting gym. I asked her about the program and its cost, and she informed me that I would love it. Amy and I had always had good conversations when we were together, and I enjoyed her energy.

"You should come with me to class some night! I bet you'll love it," she told me as one of her kids climbed onto her lap. A couple of days later, she picked me up and we headed down the hill to the gym. She was right—I loved it. Not being able to compete in sports growing up crushed me and it felt good to finally have an outlet. I had always been an active person, but my food choices always outweighed any workouts I had done. We arrived at the gym and the energy was intoxicating. We completed the workout and my body felt like it was on a high.

I craved more and signed up to become a member at New Castle Gym. For five nights a week, I was in the gym. I made friends quickly and lifted heavier even quicker.

As the timer beeped to start our workout, everything else around me faded away. It was just me and my barbell, and I wanted to be the first one done every time. It felt good to throw around heavy weight, to push myself to the limits. There was something inside me that fueled this type of focus, and I didn't quite know what it was yet. It felt good to be sore and not let it slow me down.

My body was getting stronger, and several times, the coach

would comment on my new abs or my biceps. I was constantly crushing my personal records and soon I even started hosting classes. The community at the gym was so encouraging and happy, I loved the energy in the gym. It became my second home—until the night I ran out, never to return.

It was just another night at the gym and everyone was setting up their stations for the workout. I was pumped up as I danced next to my barbell to the pounding music.

"Stations ready! Let's go!" Coach yelled as the timer started. This workout consisted of box jumps, pull-ups, sprints, and a lift called "snatch." I hated this lift and constantly struggled with it, but I didn't let that slow me down. The music brought great energy to the class as everyone around me worked so hard, sweat puddles soon scattered around the gym floor. I hammered out my pull-ups, box jumps, the sprint, then it was time to get that damn bar up and over my head.

"Let's go, Draya! You got this! You're strong, let's see it!" The coach encouraged me, for he knew I struggled with this lift.

Finding my position at the bar, I went in for the lift and couldn't get it past my head.

"You've got this! Try again!" coach was in my face, screaming at me now. Taking a breath, I tried again but failed. For what seemed to be an eternity, I tried over and over to get that bar above my head, but I couldn't. I started doubting myself and looking around I saw the class was finishing their workouts, wiping sweat from their faces and giving each other high-fives, yet here I was, still on my first round, struggling to get the bar over my head. I felt as though the weight of the world was on my shoulders. I was embarrassed, I felt weak, and I was ashamed of myself. I always finished first, but not today.

Soon the entire class started cheering me on as they cleaned up their stations. There was so much encouragement and positivity encompassing the gym, but all I felt was shame. I felt the tears coming and knew I couldn't stop them. I threw the barbell down, jumped over it, and ran out of the gym.

The cold winter air hit my face, snapping me back to reality. I threw my head back and took in several big breaths, soaking in this moment of calm before I had to explain myself. Amy came running out of the gym, the door slamming behind her.

"What's going on?" she asked me as she handed me my water bottle and jacket.

"We need to go. I'll tell you in the car," I insisted. My head was spinning. *How can this be? How have I gone my entire life forgetting about my abuse, and why now was it constantly coming up in my memory?*

I was terrified of my future; I was terrified of having to revisit those awful memories. I felt out of control and that was something I was never good at. I felt like my entire life was a lie. I felt as if I was not only a victim to my brother but a victim to the LLC as well.

Pulling into the driveway of my house, Amy threw the car in park and asked me again, "So what's going on?"

My head fell to my hands as I wept. I couldn't bring myself to say the words, the thought alone crushed me. I was ashamed I had allowed this secret to bury itself in the deepest parts of me. The rain fell on the windshield as the windows started to fog up, and I continued to weep. Amy's hand brushed my hair and rubbed my shoulders as she so patiently instructed me to breathe and reassured me that whenever I was ready, she was there to listen.

I had never experienced such love before, such compassion. Every decision I had made in my life, every suppressed emotion, it was all surfacing here and now. My head pounded, and my shirt was drenched from my endless tears. I pulled down the passenger mirror, looking at the reflection of a girl so scared, lost, and broken.

"Something happened to me when I was young," I said as I stared at myself in the mirror.

"Do you want to talk about it?" Amy asked me.

"It was . . . it was my brother. He . . . He did horrible things to me . . . He raped me," I told Amy through my gasping sobs.

"Does anyone else know?" she asked.

"No, you're the first and only person I've told," I answered, so weak and broken.

"How old were you when it happened?"

"I was about twelve or so, I think. I can't remember much about the details I want to remember—it's the bad ones I can't seem to get rid of."

"You've got to face them, Draya. It's the only way," Amy informed me.

Reality set in, and I knew there was no going back. There was no more suppressing my emotions, no more shoving the fact that I was raped under the rug. I had some work that needed to be done, I needed to get to know the woman I saw in the mirror. I needed to heal. Hugging Amy tight and expressing my gratitude for her, I let her go home to her kids. I needed sleep, and as I curled up in my bed, I screamed into my pillow. The anger had surfaced.

Making an extra strong pot of coffee that morning, I tossed back ibuprofen for my pounding headache from crying so hard the night before. I slept the best I ever had in my entire life that night—no nightmares and no more tossing and turning.

I grabbed my phone and texted my dad while I had the courage. "Hey, I would like to talk to you about something. Can I come over for coffee tonight?"

My dad had just recently retired from his job at the local lumber mill and moved to Colorado to continue working, while Mom stayed back in Washington with my youngest sibling Abby. Abby was in her senior year of high school, and the house would go on the market after she graduated.

Making the turn onto the driveway, my headlights shone on my dad's trailer parked in my brother's driveway. My heart was racing, but for once in my life, I was consumed by courage and confidence.

Sitting down with a cup of coffee and a pastry of some sort, my Dad asked me, "So, what do you want to tell me?"

My heart ached because I knew this information would crush my dad's heart. I knew the fact that his son raped his daughter, in his home, would absolutely crush him and he would wear that guilt for far too long. I couldn't hold back the tears any longer, but I was impressed as the words seemed to come out much easier this time. I told my dad that one of the brothers had done something to me—I couldn't bring myself to use the words "molestation" and "rape." Maybe my courage wasn't as strong as I thought.

"Let's call one of the ministers, they would be a good one to talk to about this to because they always have such great advice," Dad said, a lack of expression on his face.

WHAT THE FUCK? was what I thought in my head. "Please, Dad, no. I don't want anyone else to know right now. I've got some serious work that needs to be done, and I don't think any minister is going to be able to help me." The last thing I wanted was for the preacher to be telling his wife, who then would tell everyone she knew. The gossip would break out in the LLC, and it would spread like wildfire.

The look on my dad's face was that of the face I saw so many times growing up: a look of disappointment and fear. He preached the gospel to me and told me everything was going to be okay. I asked him if he could tell Mom about this for me, and he said he would tell her when he goes to Longview for Thanksgiving in a week.

"I'd much rather tell her in person," he said.

"What about the brother that did this to me? Can you call him too?" I asked him.

"Of course," Dad responded. A wave of relief came over me. This type of communication was what I knew growing up—using forgiveness anytime something was wrong and not showing emotion. Those two together, I soon realized, was not how I would choose to live my life, nor express myself. But in that moment, with my elbows on Dad's trailer kitchen table, I felt relief.

The next few weeks went by in a blur. My dad knew about

my abuse, and I trusted him to tell my mother about this, and together they would take action in talking to my brother. Thanksgiving came and went, and I thought it was odd my mother hadn't called me or even sent me a text regarding the news Dad promised to deliver to her. Resentment started to build toward both my parents as I struggled every day to simply get through.

That month went by in a series of sleepless nights, emotional roller coasters, and suppression. I was so weak, and I felt so lost. As a victim, I can tell you that when you're at your lowest, or even when you're feeling a weight such as this, the last thing you feel you can do is ask for help. I was so damn weak and tired, I just wanted someone to take care of me, but no one was there.

So once again I buckled up and got through it, and then Mom arrived for Christmas.

"So, did Dad talk to you?" I asked her. She had been in town for a few days and I thought it strange that she hadn't given me an extra-tight hug or words of love and support.

"Oh yeah, he kind of mentioned something about something happening to you when you were young. But he said it seems like you're doing good."

I was heartbroken. What else did I have to do to get the support from my parents? My heart was screaming inside me, and my feet wanted to run. Carrying the weight of my abuse for all those years suddenly became too heavy and I couldn't help but question if my place on this earth was actually worth it.

I felt it was important for my siblings to know that my brother was a predator. I needed them to know the facts for the safety of their children. My brother claimed he was just a curious teenager, and that it wasn't a problem anymore. But I disagreed, which I still do now. When he sexually abused me, he was around sixteen to seventeen years old—old enough that he knew it was wrong. Now I was concerned about my nieces and nephews and his kids.

This fear, to this day, is still in the back of my mind. Perhaps if he would have served time in jail or paid for his sins in some other way, I would view this a little differently. But lastly, I needed to know if this had happened to anyone else in my family.

We gathered all the siblings and their wives at my parents' one evening. I could see the curiosity on their faces. Sitting next to Mom on the recliner I couldn't hold back the sobs as Dad filled everyone in on what had happened to me. We all hugged, cried, and words of support and encouragement were spoken to me. I wept happy tears, soaking in the feelings, free of judgment and full of love. This was what family was supposed to feel like.

But with each passing day after that meeting, nobody reached out and I started feeling lonely and weaker, unable to keep pushing through, and I started distancing myself from my family. Looking in the mirror one day, I told myself, *This is all on you*. My thoughts started racing, trying to convince myself that if nobody wanted to support me, then I had no other choice. I had the power within myself to be brave and courageous. I'd been on my own my entire life, why not keep it that way?

I blocked people out of my life because I was tired of waiting around for support and guidance. It was time to get to work, and I was the only one who could make that happen.

CHAPTER NINETEEN

The river is a source of power that we can never tame and we will always fear it in some capacity. When I first started working at Whitewater in 2012, I was quite the shy, timid, church girl who would leave work out the side door because the raft guides were enjoying some beers in the boathouse after their day on the river. Sounds of beer cans being opened, chugged, crushed, and then tossed in the trash had me freaking out. Coming from an upbringing where drinking was criticized and looked upon as alcoholism and addiction, I made sure I stayed away from it.

What if they asked me if I wanted one? How would I interact with them? *They clearly are drunks*, I thought to myself. I was instantly judging the situation without even being open to seeing it. I was consumed by a habit called fear, which the LLC instilled deep within me. The way ministers spoke about drinking in sermons had me conditioned to believe that it meant much more than just having a couple of beers after work.

After spending a winter serving booze on the mountain, I realized drinking was not what the LLC portrayed it to be. You can be a good person and enjoy a beverage, or two or three, and if you had four—well, that didn't necessarily make you an alcoholic.

As I went to leave the boathouse that warm spring day, I didn't even think twice about exiting through the side door.

"Draya!" my coworkers called from the inflated raft they were sitting and lounging in.

"Come join us!" Alex, one of the senior raft guides, hollered at me. There was no peer pressure to drink, and these guys weren't obviously drunk. I'm sure they knew I was a religious girl based on my vibe, but regardless, they were welcoming and nice.

As the summer went on, I had the opportunity to get on the river as an extra paddler for our double extreme trips. This was two laps down the Shoshone section of the Colorado River. Typically, when my help was needed to paddle it was because the skill set of the guest wasn't there or an odd number of guests were in the raft. I was simply there for pure muscle power, and I loved it. I started thinking about participating in training the following summer. I felt this wild unknown connection with the river, and I wanted more of it. I knew the boathouse was going to be a reoccurring summer job and I figured I might as well start hanging out and making friends because, as a matter of fact, these dirty, smelly, belly-laughing raft guides were fun to hang out with.

2014

That summer I became the full-time photographer at Whitewater, taking photos of the guests as they crashed through the Shoshone rapids! Work provided me with a five-speed, two-wheel drive, no AC, red pickup along with an old neon bike to cruise up and down the bike path with. The days were busy as I had to photograph, deliver, crop, and display the photos before the trip got back to the boathouse. I biked nearly ten miles a day and got a wicked suntan.

There was something so grounding about being next to the river. Just like the forest, it had a way of connecting me to a higher power. Being the photographer, I was able to memorize the "line" the guides would take the rafts down, which gave me an advantage in the next year's training.

Being alone all day gave me a lot of time and space to think, and the memories of abuse started to resurface again. At the beginning of the day, I resembled that of a giant pot of water on the stove, with its lid on. As the day went on, the water in the pot started to boil and soon it was bubbling out of the lid in a rage to free itself. There were days I arrived back at the boathouse and would lock myself in the photo room, editing photos through my blurry eyes. I couldn't keep my emotions at bay any longer. I was filled with rage, pain, fear, shame, and the list only went on. I couldn't place exactly how I was feeling in those moments, but I knew they were related to my childhood and that if I continued the road of avoiding help, things would get ugly.

It didn't take long for others to notice I wasn't being my usual happy self, and people started asking if I was okay. There was a moment I remember walking from the photo room to the photo display room when I caught Phoebe's eye. She could see the pain in my face and motioned for me to come into the office. Welcoming me into a big hug, she held me tight and reassured me she was here for me and if I wanted to talk, she was happy to listen. I told her about the abuse and the issues the religion brought to it. I told her how I felt so alone and scared and that my family had basically disregarded the fact that their son/brother sexually abused their daughter/sister. I felt like a ticking time bomb walking around, and with any discomfort, suggestions on how to do my job better, or criticism, I would instantly blow up.

The boathouse became a safe place for me, and I was finding excuses to not go home right away after work. This was the first time in my life I was starting to feel a true connection with people around me, and I started to look at the world through different eyes. Many times when I explain to others my religious upbringing, I often put my hands to my face, creating a tunnel-vision visual. This demonstrates how the people of the LLC see the world, and that's all I knew until now. Whitewater allowed me to take my hands down from my face, and it offered me a 360-view of the world. I decided it was time to walk away from the LLC practice. I no longer had a desire to follow this fundamental way of living, so I sent a message to my parents letting them know I will no longer be attending church or church events.

Life would only get harder from here, as I would lose my entire support group and friends. Walking through the grocery store or in town, I would occasionally cross paths with someone from the LLC or an old friend. They looked at me as if I was a stranger; they were timid, and sometimes they would avoid talking or even looking at me. I wondered if this was how everyone else in the world perceives them.

I was reborn. I was entering the world as an adult, stripped free from all the chains that used to bind me. It was an entirely new world, and I was ready to explore it.

SUMMER OF 2015: RAFT GUIDE TRAINING

Raft guide training started in May and lasted a week long. During the spring in Colorado, the weather can be quite unpredictable, and we were reminded of that while rafting in the snow, wind, rain, and sunshine, all in five days' time. Regardless of the weather, the energy was electric, and I don't think there was a time in my life when I laughed more than I did that week.

Our class was roughly twelve people, with seven being women. The first couple days of training were spent in the boathouse as we went over the daily routines and the importance of customer service. During the busy summer months, we would take nearly four hundred people down the river each day. That required impeccable teamwork and a system to follow, especially when the boathouse was full—it was like herding cats. Luckily, most of what they were teaching in training was knowledge I already had, considering I had been working at Whitewater for a few years now.

After practicing for a couple of days inflating rafts, attaching the frames, loading them onto a trailer, and tying them down, we inflated our paddle boats and got on the river. An instructor ran every raft, picking one person at a time to captain the raft downriver. Meanwhile, the instructor randomly threw volleyballs up, across, or downriver.

"Go get your swimmer," was Levi's famous words as he sat in his dry suit comfortably next to the person steering the boat. The thing about having Levi as your instructor for the day was he threw a lot of balls into the river. He kept us on our toes, he made us work as a team, and after a couple of days learning about currents and eddies, we were working effectively as a team.

"Left side forward, right side back, and all forward! Let's go get that kid swimming," I confidently shouted at my crew as I used my paddle in the back as a rudder to make small corrections as the fellow rookies paddled across the river quickly, picking up the ball, a.k.a. "the child."

"Work smarter, not harder" was one of the boathouse's mantras, and we applied that on the river and in the boathouse. Now that we had our basic river skills dialed in, and with fifty instructor miles under our belts, we were eligible to check out, on the downriver section. This meant a senior guide would row your raft through the two miles of class-III rapids and as soon as we cleared the last rapid, called "Maneater," it was time to switch spots. The rookie now was on the oars, in charge of steering the boat, keeping the guest safe, and making sure they were having a good time. If you were able to do that and show strong and smart boatmanship, you passed and were then able to guide trips downriver.

Learning to raft on moving water, and letting it do most of the work for you, was something I very quickly felt connected with. A connection unlike any other, where you must be one with the river, as it has the power you could never compete against. It was time to step up our training. This is what we had been working toward this entire time. It was time to row the oar frame's down Shoshone, a two-mile stretch of class-III rapids.

Before getting on the water, Caleb, the lead guide, walked us down the bike path as he went over each rapid in detail on how to safely set up and maneuver through. Each rapid was made up of different rock placements and shorelines, creating a rapid so unique unlike any other. "Baptism," "Eddie out Rock," "Tuttle's Tumble," "Marty's Diner," "Pinball," "The Wall," "All-Day Wave," "Blender," "Tombstone," and "Man-eater"—these were the rapids we had to learn, and in order to pass, we needed to do two things: First, we had to safely navigate the raft down the rapids, using paddle commands and giving instructions to our fellow rookies as if they were customers. Second, we had to run another lap safely down the rapids without any paddle power at all. We would have to use the river to our advantage, to be able to row a raft full of guests who can't paddle worth shit, because that would, has, and does happen on the river, all the time.

Having been the photographer for Whitewater for a couple of years now, I already knew the company line, as I'd seen it done many times. Most times the rapids were run correctly, but every so often the day got exciting, as guests would fall out of the raft, the guide could be ejected, or a raft could flip or get dump trucked, or even get pinned on rocks. I photographed what to do and what not to do in the rapids. I was feeling confident and wasted no time getting on the oars.

As we pushed off the boat ramp the feeling inside me was so powerful and empowering. For the first time in my life, I was taking charge, and as I called commands to my fellow rookies, and as we crashed through the rapids together, the river told me I was going to be okay and that I could face any challenge that came my way.

Then it was time for my second lap—the final test of training. I needed to prove I was capable of guiding guests down the river without any help, and I absolutely crushed it. I moved with the slower currents when I needed time to set up for a rapid ahead, and I pushed hard using my shoulders, core, and legs, bracing all my weight forward as I pushed through each wave. Rolling with the punches, one wave at a time, just like we do in life.

There's something to be said about wild places that have always drawn me in, whether that was the forest, the mountain, the desert, or the rivers. They have a way of putting us in our place and humbling us in ways nothing else can. The mountains don't care if you're tired when hiking or cold when a storm comes in; the river could care less if you wore a life jacket when rafting or shoes on your feet to keep them protected; the desert doesn't care if you didn't bring sunscreen or got a cactus in your foot. These beautiful places can be very dangerous if we don't respect them. These places have a way of testing us and often bring out the character in us along the way. I would learn a lot about that later down the road when I was a boat captain on a fourteen-day Grand Canyon River trip.

CHAPTER TWENTY

The relationship with my family at this point was nearly non-existent. They were sad for me and my life choices and often expressed to me that they held me in their prayers and sometimes I would even get a message with a recording from a Sunday morning sermon. They were disappointed in my life choices because of what they saw on social media. In return, I pushed them away, knowing my brother got the get-out-of-jail-free card because he believed his sins were forgiven and remained in the LLC. Meanwhile, I was the bad child running wild.

What they didn't see was the connection I had with the river, the connections I was making with people who supported my journey of healing and self-discovery. They didn't see the confidence and self-love I had gained—when I left the LLC, I nearly had none. I found it extremely difficult to communicate with my family because their religious beliefs always brought a barrier between us and, several times, caused me to leave my parents' house mid-argument.

"You just don't understand, because you have lost the Holy Spirit," they would tell me.

All I wanted was love and acceptance for my new journey in life and I felt like I was constantly fighting to receive that. And so, I pushed them away and focused on the new family I had found in the Whitewater community.

"Hey, Draya!" one of the senior guides called from across the boathouse.

"Yeah, what's up?" I asked.

"Do you want to take over the social board?" they asked me.

"I would love to!" I said as I grabbed the whiteboard leaning against the wall and started erasing it. The board looked something like this: Tuesday nights were dedicated to ultimate frisbee at the park with the other rafting companies; Wednesday was music in the park followed by cheap beers and games at a local hotel; Friday was first Fridays in Carbondale, where we would dance the night away. The rest of the week was spent rafting with coworkers after work, surfing the man-made wave with anything that floated, slides on the boat ramp, movie nights, potlucks, bowling, camping, or going to the rodeo. There was always something going on, and by the end of the summer, we all had a book of memories and friends we called family. The owners at the time, supported our active and adventurous lifestyle, and many times we would pile into a bus to go bowling or in a van to go run different stretches of rivers.

The Fourth of July tradition was to raft down the river, starting at the Shoshone boat ramp and floating down toward Two Rivers Park where we would watch the fireworks, then continue down to the boathouse late into the night. This year, we decided to take *The Spirit,* a twenty-foot bucket boat. A bucket boat has no drain holes which means someone must bucket water out as you go through the rapids. If the water isn't bailed out of the raft, it becomes too heavy to control.

We all arrived at the boat ramp with a stoke-level-ten attitude on this adventure ahead. With liquid courage in most of us, we pushed off the ramp. The first wave hit us, and it turned into chaos. Everyone was yipping and hollering, trusting the few people paddling and the guides in the back to take us downriver. I was sitting near the back, a beer in my hand, with red and blue face paint on, putting me in the perfect position to see everything that was about to go down. The senior guides behind us were screaming loud, giving paddle commands, but at this point, everyone was liquored up.

Their plan was to split Marty's Diner rapid, but with so much water and people in the raft, it was a lot heavier than they anticipated. This massive twenty-foot raft with fifteen people weighed more than a thousand pounds, and it was picking up speed. As we entered the split of Marty's Diner, the right side of the raft hit the hole of the rapid. These are the kind of holes on the river you want to avoid, as they will flip your raft, and as the water underneath recirculates back up, it will hold anyone or anything in it, tossing you around like a drying machine.

As the right tube of *The Spirit* hit the hole, the entire front of the raft folded back. This is what we call a taco. The entire crew that sat up front was now in the river. It just so happened to be a high-water year, and the river was moving quickly. We had lost all but three paddles and both buckets. *The Spirit* was now a twenty-foot swimming pool, floating downriver on its own course.

Doing our best to stay in the raft, we continued to get tossed around as the rapids crashed in. We did our best to hold on as we rode the river's wild and wet roller coaster. The guides who had gotten launched out of the boat were on their own and had to perform self-rescue. Luckily all the guides made it out safely before having to swim the wall of screaming death and dismemberment, a series of giant holes on the right side of the river would offer a gnarly swim and, luckily, we all avoided it. It was a great reality check for all of us, reminding us just how powerful the river was but also reassuring us of our skills, of self-rescue, and going with the punches.

We all regrouped at Grizzly Creek, as the thrill of what just happened brought excitement and a humbling to each one of us. This was a story we would tell for years. A once-in-a-lifetime experience that had us all high on life. We pushed off and made it to the park just in time for the fireworks to bring light and color to the town we had all fallen in love with.

Most days after work, we would go out and enjoy the river for ourselves, whether under a full moon or the warm evening sun. The time on the water reminded us why we were raft guides in the first place and allowed us to connect as friends. One of my favorite volunteer-training days was taking a raft downriver from the boathouse at high water and intentionally flipping our raft over and over in a rapid called "Dinosaur." We would call the fire station and let them know of our intentions of flipping a boat, knowing people driving along the interstate would call in the incident. A safety boat would sit just downriver of the rapid, ready in case we needed help. Round after round, we entered the rapid, sometimes sideways, sometimes all leaning to the low side, causing the raft to flip over. The objective was to flip the raft, turn it upright, and get everyone back into it before the boat ramp just a few hundred yards below the crashing hole in the river. Each time, we succeeded and worked effectively as a team to do so. We were high on life and the river brought out the childlike ways as we swam with its current.

Moving into the upstairs apartment of Whitewater I lived and breathed being a raft guide. My work was my home, and I embraced this new family and adventurous river life I was thriving in. Some early summer mornings, a select few of us would load up inflatable kayaks and drive upriver to the Grizzly Creek boat ramp and enjoy the morning floating down, watching the sun bring golden light to the canyon walls. By the end of the day, many of us had put twenty-plus miles on the river, our bodies strong and shaped from lifting and rowing rafts all day.

The transformations from the spring to the end of the season were jaw-dropping. It was always exciting seeing the new guides come in for the season and watching them grow as individuals.

There are far too many memories to share from my ten summers at Whitewater, for it was and is a special place to many of us who walked through the doors of the boathouse. I have been incredibly lucky to have gained some incredible friendships from my time there, and I know this is the case for many. The boathouse, and the river—they changed my life, but more importantly, they saved my life. When I lost everything, the boathouse was the place that welcomed me in. In ten summers, I experienced growth that was needed to find myself, and I am so grateful for every connection and moment the river gave me. People used to tell me, "Your twenties are for living," and that's exactly what we were all doing—we were living.

CHAPTER TWENTY-ONE

Despite the new self-discovery and confidence the river and boathouse gave me, drinking had become my escape, and as the four o'clock hour went off, I was cracking cold ones every day. Drinking made me forget about family issues, it made me forget about my abuse, and instead of feeling insecure, it made me feel confident. I wasn't just having a beer after work to decompress from the day, I was drinking from four p.m. till the bars closed. By the end of the night, my well-earned tip money from the day would be gone. It's what everyone else was doing, and I was fitting in just fine.

It didn't take long until I got the nickname "Rumspringa." (Rumspringa is when an Amish teenager turns eighteen and they have a full year to experience the world, and at the end of the year they have to decide whether to go back to Amish life or not. If they didn't, they would be banned for life.)

Most people start drinking and lose their virginity in their teens, and by the time they were my age, they were veterans of the drinking games. But being so new and eager it didn't take long until I was blasted drunk. That summer, I gained roughly ten pounds from drinking and eating unhealthy foods every day. Sure, I was burning an excessive number of calories on the river while guiding, but not enough to keep up with the eight oz curls.

It was a Wednesday night after music in the park when we raft guides wandered over to a local hotel to drink for cheap, sing karaoke, and play games.

The guy I was seeing at the time was sitting at the bar with another raft guide, stroking her back, his eyes squinty with drunk desire as he grinned at her. Time stood still as I sat there watching my lover hit on another woman. I felt used; I felt unwanted and unworthy. I was angry with myself that I allowed my guard to come down, and I was angry at this man for his actions. All the nights we had spent together, the quiet moments next to the river in the moonlight as we talked for hours, the affection he gave me and his listening ears—it was all for nothing.

I turned and ran out of the bar. As I ran across the crosswalk, I didn't even bother looking to see if there were any cars. My two girlfriends ran behind me, hollering at me to stop. But I kept running, just like I did when I was a young girl. I ran toward the park where we had seen music a few hours prior and fell to the ground. It was as if someone kicked me right in the gut.

My fist pounded the ground as I screamed, and I cried. All the men I had slept with, all the drinking and drugs I had been doing, it was all for nothing. It was just another bandage to cover up my wounds, just like the forgiveness was growing up. Those temporary feelings I had when intoxicated didn't matter in the real world.

I was so tired of trying, I was so tired of running away from my past that continued to haunt me. I knew the future of healing would require strength and persistence, but I feared I didn't have it within me to do so. I was tired of looking for validation and, in the end, being used. I felt everything I had been suppressing as I lay in the park that morning at two a.m.

I had hit rock bottom. My past was too fast for my tired feet, and it had caught up with me. I was ashamed of myself for letting this issue stay hidden, tucked deep under my heart, and for not getting help when the memories started coming back. It was time to seek professional help.

The next day, I called a therapist and my hands shook as I dialed her number, knowing my life was about to change, but my heart felt a sense of relief knowing healing was on its way.

Waiting outside of Annie's office, I couldn't sit still so I paced around the lobby, trying to control my nerves. I couldn't believe this was happening, that after fifteen years I would finally speak my truth and unfold the many years of misery, and for a moment that fear came back into my heart and I wanted to run out of the brick building. Taking in a big breath, I sat down on the sofa because I knew if I ran out, I would regret it for the rest of my life. *No more running*, I told myself.

The doors opened and there she stood, a stranger to me then but soon she would change my life. With open arms, she embraced me and welcomed me into her space. We got right to it as I wasted no time telling her my story. She informed me she had some knowledge of the religion I grew up in, from previous clients, which was reassuring.

Through weeping breaths, I told her everything, my eyes puffy and red as I nearly emptied the tissue box Annie placed next to me. That first session was spent filling Annie in on my story, and as each session came and went, we dug deeper into my healing. I wanted to press charges against my brother but unfortunately, the state of Washington has a statute of limitations of ten years. I had just missed the mark and legally I couldn't do anything.

I felt I needed to call him, to confront him about his mistakes, and courageously, I picked up the phone and sent him a message asking if he was free to chat. My heart raced and my face became hot as I hit send. He replied quickly and we set up a time to chat later that day. He informed me he remembered the moments of abuse, that he was sorry, and that he was just a curious teenager. He asked for his forgiveness, and I told him I couldn't forgive him in the way I used to (using the LLC gospel), but that I could forgive him in my own way. I wanted so badly to move on quickly and I thought if I forgave my brother then and there, things would get better. I wanted the pain, the memories, I wanted all of it to go away, and so I told myself I had to forgive him. Turns out as I progressed in my healing and started looking into my unhealthy mental state and my way of coping, I realized I hadn't forgiven him, and it would take me years of self-healing to do so.

I never was a writer growing up nor did I have a desire to do so, but one afternoon, Annie assigned me homework for the two weeks until I saw her next. She instructed me that anytime I was feeling an emotion, to sit with it, to really feel it, and ask myself, "Why am I feeling this way? What's causing me to feel this way? How can I change things, so I don't feel this anymore?" After taking a moment to sit with my feelings, I was to pick up a pen and paper and write about it. This was by far the best advice I received from Annie, as writing has been a tool for me to help process emotion, life changes, and even communicating with others. I encourage you to pick up a pen and write. It can be as simple as what you did that day, a description of a memory, your goals, how something made you feel, your wildest dreams, whatever it may be.

Over time, it became apparent which emotions I was feeling most, as I would go back and read my journaling. I felt I was suddenly holding myself accountable for whatever was happening and checking in with my mental state of mind. Writing started to redirect my life as I began to work out again and took a much-needed break from drinking. I was determined to change my coping habits and to focus on myself, in a healthy way. I decided to sign up for a half marathon, set for the following summer. It was time to start training. It was time to start running.

RACE DAY

I felt strong going into race day, and I told myself this wasn't going to be a race I was trying to win but more so a challenge for myself. I had never competed in a race before, and I made it my goal to complete the 13.1 miles in under four hours.

Looking around at the runners who surrounded me, they were clearly skilled athletes. Their short shorts exposed their lean, muscular legs and I could tell they had been doing this for years. The energy was electric as race numbers were handed out and attached to shirts, the runners stretched and drank from their water bottles. We took a bus ride up the windy road to where they would drop us off, just below Ruedi Reservoir. The course would take us downhill, along the Frying Pan River, as we passed many farming fields with cows and horses feeding in the tall wispy green grass, the red canyons and cliffs bringing a colorful backdrop to it all. It was a beautiful warm day as a cool breeze came up the river.

It was time to line up and start the race. I found my place toward the back of the crowd, letting the skilled runners have their place up front. I ran with my friend Joanie who had run several races before, and soon she picked up her stride and left me in the dust. I felt strong as I kept a slower pace, not wanting to go too hard and lose my endurance.

As I ran, I thought about my life from the moment I was born leading up to the present moment. Memories from my childhood that I had forgotten suddenly resurfaced, like the times my uncle Gordy came over and I would hide behind the couch because I was scared of him. He stood there hovering over the couch handing me a chocolate bar, luring me out from my hiding place. I remembered those uneasy feelings from when my brother's friend stayed at our house, because for some reason he creeped me out. Turns out, years later, he got charged for the molestation of twelve-plus kids. I thought about all the times I was strong and brave as I wandered the forest, hunting alone, and through those sleepless nights when I was consumed by my nightmares. I thought about the sad girl I was in my teenage years, lost in a fog as I went through the motions of everyday life.

Suddenly a runner's high came over me as I thought about that night, I hit rock bottom and just how far I had come. I was healing, I was getting stronger every day, and with every step, I ran further away from my past and closer to my bright future.

Mile marker seven and the hydration station suddenly appeared in front of me, bringing a smile to my face. I grabbed a quick shot of electrolytes from the smiling woman in a bright-pink hoodie and kept running.

My legs began to feel heavy, and my mental state had become foggy, as I reached mile marker eleven. My goal of finishing the race in under four hours now shifted simply to "keep on running." Walking was no longer an option. To achieve this goal, I needed to tap into my younger self, that girl who so easily ran away.

Slowing my pace, I forced myself to replay those traumatic moments when my brother sexually abused me. I held so much anger inside toward him and I remembered the pain from that day he raped me. I told myself over and over, "No pain will ever compare to what he inflicted on you."

My feet hammered on the sidewalk as I let my anger fuel me to finish the race, and before I knew it, I was making my way down the final stretch along the main street. Cheering and encouragement came from strangers, those lined up behind the orange cones, and a chill came over me as I turned the corner.

I saw the finish line. Tears ran down my sweaty cheeks as I charged forward, and as I crossed that line, there were no friends or family there to embrace me in my success. There, all alone, I soaked it in. A moment so intimate with myself, a moment of discovering the woman I was becoming. I was shedding the layers of my old self and empowered by my finish time of two hours and thirty-eight minutes.

CHAPTER TWENTY-TWO

It was a cold November morning when I hit the trailhead well before sunrise. My heavy breathing brought fog to the cold air, making the trail difficult to see. I had ventured out a few times now on solo hunts but hadn't notched a tag yet. I was headed to an area that always had deer, and I was hopeful as I hiked the three miles to the area I was planning to hunt. I've always been a fan of hiking earlier in the morning than later, for it's better to be waiting for the sun to rise versus getting to a spot after your kill window has passed.

I used an old telephone road to access the area I wanted to be at just before first light. Taking a right where the road forked, I slowly walked, keeping my eyes up scanning for movement or white butts feeding among the thicket. The ground had a layer of frost, making it difficult to walk quietly on the crunchy dirt, and the leaves that had fallen.

I planned to sit in a field that sat above some private land, roughly a few hundred yards up the hill, a spot where deer typically moved through in the morning as they left the fields to go to bed. A well-used game trail crossed the open space in front of me reassuring me this was a good area to sit and wait.

My nose was red from the cool temperature. The sky was bright pink as the sun came up over the mountains, and everything around me had a warm glow to it. It was a magical moment now ingrained in my memory.

Movement to my left caught the corner of my eye, and I saw a great buck walking along the well-used trail. He was headed for private land in search of a doe. As he walked, he strutted like that of a high school quarterback on prom night. He licked his lips as he strutted, most likely smelling a doe not too far off. Dropping my butt to the ground, I pulled my knees up, resting my elbows on them, and settled the .300 mag tight to my shoulder. Seeing my movement, the buck stopped perfectly broadside at just under one hundred yards. Taking aim, I slowly squeeze the trigger, dropping the buck dead in his tracks.

My heart pounded loud in my chest. The sunrise was in all her glory as everything glowed vibrantly and warmly around me. A smile filled my face as a few tears rolled down my cold cheeks! Walking up to the buck, I was blown away at how beautiful he was. His thick antlers were dark brown, and he had a kicker off the right side. A hole in the left side of his main beam told the story of another hunter who tried to kill him. Luckily, they missed, leaving him for me.

As I looked down at this beautiful animal, it hit me all at once. Dad wasn't here to help, or anyone else—it was just me. A smile spread across my face and I knew I had the skills to get this job done all alone. I had seen my dad field dress many animals, and most times I helped as I held a leg and transferred chunks of meat to the game bags nearby.

Wasting no time, I made quick work of quartering and grabbing his back straps and tenderloins. The carcass and guts would feed the birds, coyotes, bears, and insects, and I couldn't wait till dinner when I would feast on fresh organic meat, found, killed, and processed by me. Finishing in just under a couple hours, the sun was warming the earth now and I knew I needed to get this meat to a cooler place.

I grabbed each game bag and stuffed them into my pack, not wanting to come back for a second trip. Deep inside me, I knew this hunt was a test on how hard I could push myself. *Could I pack this entire deer out in one shot?* I asked myself. Dropping to the ground, I put the straps of my pack around my shoulders and tightened everything down. After several attempts, I was finally able to stand up with nearly 150 pounds on my back. Slinging my dad's .300 mag over my shoulder, I took the first steps toward a new version of myself.

My steps started getting heavy only a few hundred yards from where I had killed this buck. I was nearly three miles from the truck, and this was just the start of it. I knew I needed to dig in deep and mentally get my shit together. Luckily, the adrenaline helped as I stumbled a hundred yards at a time, telling myself, *Slow and steady wins the race.*

As the sweat dripped from my forehead, I thought about the young girl I used to be. I thought about that day in the cabin and was reminded of the pain I suffered as my brother raped me. A burst of energy came through me and I told myself, *This is nothing like the pain you've experienced before. Keep going, this pain is just temporary.* And so, with each step through the grass and rocks, I thought about those moments when I wanted to be strong but failed to do so. I thought about the pain and how nothing could stop me now.

I felt invincible, I felt courageous, brave, and strong, but most importantly, I felt in control. Tears once again flowed down my cheeks, and before I knew it, the truck was in sight. Dropping the tailgate on my truck, I let my heavy pack rest as I unstrapped it and freed myself from it. My body buzzed on a high of adrenaline and pride, and I knew this hunt had changed me. I could feel it in the deepest parts of me. I didn't know exactly what it was, but I knew my future, the one I had dreamed of forever, was now in motion and I couldn't wait to see where that was going to bring me.

CHAPTER TWENTY-THREE

Amy and I, two pretty blondes with giddy smiles on our faces, made our way to the bar called The Springs. Tonight, we wanted to celebrate my success in harvesting my buck and for the mental breakthroughs I had experienced on that hunt. We were just two gals looking to catch up at the bar. There had never been any shortage of conversation between Amy and me, as we both seemed to be on the same wavelengths in life. Amy and I both left the church around the same time and, luckily, we had each other to process the shift in our lives that so suddenly happened.

We sipped on our whiskey and laughed our faces off as we caught up on life. Wandering eyes from the men behind the bar annoyed us; it seemed like every man in the room was trying to buy us a drink or talk with us. A young man with a red beard and a beanie covering his long red hair walked up asking us if we wanted to play a game of pool. Looking at each other, we decided why not.

Grabbing fresh drinks, we made our way to the pool table as the guys racked the balls for the next game. "Hey, I'm Pat, and I'm Bill," the two handsome men introduced themselves. The energy was good between the four of us, as we comfortably talked about who we were.

"We're hunting guides currently on a break in-between seasons right now; we guide up at Timber Bench Outfitters," Bill informs us.

"No way! Draya, tell them about the buck you just killed!" Amy exclaimed and then insisted.

Acting like it was no big deal, I told Bill and Pat about the buck I had just harvested a couple of days back. After showing them photos and telling the story, the guys were impressed with my skill and ambition to get after it.

"You should come work with us!" Bill and Pat both told me.

I was blown away. "Are you serious?" I asked, surprised. With only the fourth season left of hunting season, they told me they would tell their boss about me and that next year I totally should work with them.

"We'd love to have you up there, plus it would be good to have a girl in camp."

I was pumped up—this was something I'd always wanted to do, and now the opportunity was right in front of me. Next year's hunting season couldn't get here fast enough.

That year came and went just like most do and it was time to chase elk in the mountains. Becoming a hunting guide was a big deal for me, as this was literally my childhood dream, and so I dedicated the entire month of September to pursuing elk and learning about their habitat and their habits.

I packed up the pickup with a month's worth of supplies and headed to my favorite place. I knew in order to be a guide, I needed to take some time to learn as much as I could and hopefully, in the process, I could fill my tag. I'd never been one to do things half-assed and I wanted to become the best guide I could be—and to do so, I needed to put in some work. Having grown up in a hunting family, I already had a wealth of knowledge under my belt, but I knew I needed more.

My heart was happy as I drove to camp, listening to country music and singing along as I tapped the steering wheel. I was more than ready to decompress from the world and the responsibilities we seem to acquire. I had spent a good amount of time hunting solo throughout my life, but nothing to the extent of this. My family would hunt on the weekends, and it was always lovely to have the camaraderie around, but most of the time it was just me.

I was so timid and nervous when I first arrived at the hunting camp, as I carried my 9mm pistol on my hip, constantly watching my back for black bears or a mountain lion. When night fell upon me, I felt defenseless and small but would distract myself with daydreams of chasing elk.

One night, I couldn't fall asleep when a noise outside of the tent had me nervous. I instantly assumed it was a bear sniffing around the base of the tent, and my heart started to race. After a while, my curiosity got the best of me and I had to check to see what was outside my tent. Grabbing my pistol and headlamp I looked out and saw nothing. Back in the tent, I heard the noise again, and so once again, I got up to look but saw nothing.

I woke the next morning realizing it was just a field mouse that was cruising around the bottom of the tent, not a bear. Silly to think this was how I'd react, right? What would you think as you lay in bed at night, all alone in the mountains for the first time, while noises came from outside the tent? After that night, the worries that crept in at night seemed to fade away as I became more comfortable with being alone in the dark. But this was just the start of uncomfortable situations that would play out during that month in the mountains.

One afternoon, I was nearly to the top of the flattops, learning some new country. Wild raspberries littered the meadows, and as I walked through them, I feasted on the sweet red berry. In search of a water hole nearby, I kept slowly moving but not turning up any fresh signs. Reaching a patch of aspens, I stopped in my tracks upon hearing a high pitch noise. Thinking it was that of an elk bugling, I listened. The hair on the back of my neck stood up and chills ran through my body as two mountain lions screamed back and forth. They were within a hundred yards of me and the last thing I wanted was to be in the middle of two cats either breeding or defending their territory.

Not thinking, just acting, I took off, wanting to put some distance between the cats and me. After a little while, I noticed the terrain around me wasn't familiar. Pulling up my map I realized

I went the opposite way of where I was trying to go. To get back to camp, I had to backtrack past the cats. I decided to drop in elevation, out of sight of the cats, and in doing so I jumped a big bull from his bed. I made myself sit down and go over the situation that just played out. I took some deep breaths and calmed myself. I overreacted and managed to spook a bull that was in the area. Fear took over me when I heard the cats screaming, and I didn't stop and think about my direction. Maintaining your composure when in situations like this would take time to learn, and they would make you a more confident hunter.

The next morning, I made my way to a series of meadows we had seen elk in before. After hiking two and a half miles in the dark, I got to where I wanted to be for dawn, and I blew out a bugle. Instantly, I get two responses and I headed in their direction. As I slowly made my way through the aspens and firs, I could hear the two bulls screaming back and forth to each other. I checked the wind, and it was in my favor. I continued to close the distance hoping I could get between both bulls as they fought for their place in the harem. Approaching a small meadow, I waited, looked, and listened but I still could not see any elk. I let out a couple cow calls, then proceeded forward, hoping I could get twenty to forty yards past where I called. This is where I made my mistake.

As I walked through the meadow, I saw the bull coming toward me. I stopped at the lone fir tree in the middle of the meadow and knocked an arrow. As the bull came to the edge of the meadow, he was just forty yards from me, but I was unable to pull back since he had me pinned down. "Shoot," I mumbled under my breath, knowing exactly what I did wrong in this situation. I should have walked the outside edge of the meadow so that way when he walked to his doorway, I potentially could have had a shot. As the bull ran off, another lesson was learned in the elk woods, yet I experienced something so wild only so few people in this world got the pleasure of doing so.

That month, I learned lesson after lesson. Not having someone there to take charge or to bounce ideas off, I was on my own, each mistake I made was on me. I loved it; I felt as if I was growing not only as a hunter but as an individual. I felt a deep sense of connection and purpose. It was like I had discovered a new lease on life, one I had been searching for for a long time.

One afternoon, I decided to sit by a water hole that I knew the elk used. Not feeling confident in my setup, I decided to move down the hill just thirty yards from the water hole. Just as I was getting settled into the new spot, I caught movement from the corner of my eye. A cow and a giant six-by-six bull were feeding right through where I had just been sitting! If only I would have stayed there, I would most likely have gotten a shot. I notched an arrow, my heart racing, hoping they would feed closer to me. The bull's antlers were massive, and as he walked through the aspen grove, he tilted his head this way and that, maneuvering so smoothly through the narrow white trees. It was a moment in time I will remember forever—I was in their home, but they had no idea I was there. I watched them for a good hour or so, not able to get a shot but ecstatic about what I just experienced.

My dad and older sister arrived at camp on a Friday evening, and it felt good to have company after hunting solo for several days. The three of us had hunted together for years now and had created quite the team and bond. As we sat around the fire cooking steaks, I filled them in on this big bull I saw a couple of days before, and we made a plan for our hunt the next day.

We left camp the next morning just before daylight, making our way to a basin just below where I'd seen the big bull. We set up and let out a couple cow calls, followed by a bugle, and a few minutes later got a response. We had hunted this area for a few years now and had gotten to know the little honey holes and pockets that these elk hid in.

The foliage was thick, and the hillside was steep as we made our way down to work this bull that just responded to our calls. When hunting, especially with a bow, you have two factors that you always have to work against—the wind and thermals. Thermals means when the day warms up, your scent will naturally rise up the landscape as well. When evening hits and the air cools off, your scent will also naturally travel downhill. Once we got into position, using the thermals in our favor, the elk had gone quiet. They either smelled us, heard us, saw us, or simply moved on.

We enjoyed a cup of coffee and a snack as we listened in hopes the elk were still close by. The morning sun started to warm the earth, and we threw our packs on and continued to move up the mountain. As the thermals change in the mornings and evenings, it is important to be in a position where your scent doesn't go up or downhill to where the elk are bedded down or feeding. With one smell of a human the elk will spook before you have a chance of seeing them.

Making a big half circle, we looped around to where we wanted to spend the afternoon and, in doing so, jumped a herd of elk. Checking the wind, we decided to wait a little longer, or at least until the thermals were consistent.

Archery hunting can be action-packed, or it can turn into a waiting game, and this hunt turned into a waiting game. The afternoon sun was hot as we napped under a big fir tree.

"Give a bugle, let's keep that bull interested," Dad told me, and sure enough, in response to my bugle, the big bull screamed back from his bed.

We had been hunting this bull for the past couple of years, but never had an opportunity for a shot. He was truly a ghost of the forest, as he would always bugle from his bed or the dark thick timber, not wanting to expose himself, letting us know he was the king of the mountain. After our afternoon nap, we checked our wind and slowly moved in, above the timber this bull was bedded in. We reached our point of setting up and let out a couple more calls.

BOOM!

A muzzleloader cap went off, but not the powder. Weird. We all looked at each other, shrugging our shoulders. Then, it went off again. Even weirder. Was this hunter intentionally trying to push this bull away from us? Hearing something crashing through the thick timber, we knocked an arrow just in case an elk appeared in front of us.

Instead, a man in blue jeans and a flannel came stomping through the trees, no orange vest or hat on. We waved at him, hoping he would come over and chat with us, but he continued stomping his way out of the woods. As hunters, we sure love our public lands but it's unfortunate when other hunters ruin a hunt you've put so much work into.

Annoyed, we figured this hunter scared the elk out and so we decided to slowly work our way through the timber toward a series of meadows we thought the elk may have gotten pushed to. Rubs covered nearly every tree, and beds and piles of elk scat littered the hillside. The smell of elk urine and bull piss brought an overwhelming stench, and we knew we were close as we were literally standing in their bedroom.

Ever so slowly we crept through the elk-infested hillside, knowing it was just a matter of time until we bumped into them. Looking back at Dad, I motioned him to bugle and so he did. A scream from the forest let us know the big bull was close and he was closing the distance. No words were spoken between us three as Bridgette and I took off to set up, and my dad dropped back to call.

This bull was pissed off knowing there was another bull in his bedroom, and he was ready to fight. I heard crashing and a series of cow calls above me, and I knew they were headed right for Bridgette.

The bull ran twenty yards and stopped broadside right in front of her.

Thwack! She made a perfect shot! Walking up to the sister I looked up to for so long, she had the biggest smile on her face. We hugged in this moment we had rarely experienced. Moments such as this seem to be impossible to describe to someone who isn't a hunter. A bond was created in this moment unlike any I have ever found.

The three of us have hunted together ever since my sister and I were young girls, many times our hunts ended in not filling our tag. The smiles on our faces this time said it all as we worked together, cutting away at the meat as it moved through limited hands, processed by ourselves. The connection to our meat was full of emotion, hard work, and a deep appreciation attached to it.

The rainstorm that passed through just after my sister shot her bull created muddy and slippery conditions. With at least a hundred pounds of meat on each of our backs, we had our fair share of slips and falls. Our bodies had become conditioned to this type of work though, and each time we fell, our heavy packs made it difficult to get back up, but we giggled and talked about how we looked forward to our delicious dinner ahead of us.

I took a couple days to do laundry and resupply on food before heading back out to hunting camp with my brother Allan. Allan and I had this luck that seemed to follow us when hunting, as we always saw animals. We were hopeful this was the case as we hunted an area we called the "honey hole."

The morning was quiet as we sat on a meadow that the elk would feed on frequently. I wanted to wait for the thermals to switch before we headed toward the area my sister shot her bull a few days back. I knew there were more bulls in this spot, and at this point, I was happy with shooting a cow. It didn't take long until the warm September day forced the thermals to move uphill, and just like that we were on the move.

My younger brother was new to calling elk, but he was excited to follow along on this hunt as the caller. We made our way along a well-used game trail that wrapped around the ridge. Just as I came around the bend on the trail, I spotted two small bulls feeding along the side of the ridge, and I motioned to my brother to move back into the timber to make a few cow calls, just enough to pull these young, curious bulls closer for a shot.

Squatting down and using the foliage to cover my outline and movements, I took a few steps off the tail as Allan started calling forty yards behind me. These young elk were curious and wanted to spread their seed to ensure their genetics for future generations. I used my range finder which told me how far the tree was they were about to pass and took a deep breath. I had been struggling this season with maintaining my composure when in proximity to a bull, but this time, I was calm. I felt ready.

Pulling back my bow, I anchored just as I had practiced, and I settled my pin. My arrow flew in slow motion as I watched its impact. It hit right where I aimed, right behind the shoulder. I covered my mouth in disbelief, almost surprised that I had made such a great shot. I had been hunting hard for twenty-five days, and in those twenty-five days, I made many mistakes—but finally, it all came through.

We struggled to find a blood trail, creating an uneasy feeling inside my stomach, but soon I was reassured of my shot when Allan hollered at me while holding the bloody broken arrow up in the air.

As I walked up to him, I saw the broadhead was still inside the bull. A wave of relief flowed through me, and soon we found blood. No more than eighty yards from where I shot this bull, he'd fallen. No suffering was had by this bull, as within seconds of my broadhead's impact, he expired. An ethical shot, ruining no meat in the process. Walking up on the small five-by-five bull, his fifth tines still had velvet clinging on. He was a young bull, so his meat would be tender and, honestly, the best you could find.

This feeling was almost indescribable. So many miles and hours were spent in search of just finding an elk. Many mistakes were made, as I was constantly humbled by how difficult it was to harvest such a giant ghost of the forest with a bow. My body had become shaped by these mountains I explored, strong and lean, and my mind was clearer than it ever had been.

As I cut away prime meat from this bull, my purpose in life became clearer. Through these experiences I had alone in the mountains, I found a way to heal from my past trauma, embracing the courage and confidence I found as I wandered the mountainside. I had healed in a way I didn't know was possible and this wild animal was a big part of it.

"See, Draya, luck always seems to follow us when hunting together," my proud brother told me, a big smile on his face. Stepping over deadfall and through thick foliage, we made our way up the steep hill. Our heavy packs were stuffed to the brim with wild organic meat as we strapped them down to our backs. Regardless of the weight, my legs seemed to have a spring in their step, as adrenaline and accomplishment fueled the pack out back to camp.

CHAPTER TWENTY-FOUR

Archery season was over, and it was time to apply what I had learned during September to guiding. Nerves of excitement and the unknown kept me entertained as I drove over the mountain pass toward Timber Bench Outfitters.

Turning right, I made the final ascent up five miles of four-by-four gravel road. I knew life was about to change, and I could sense opportunity was on the horizon. I had dreamed of being a hunting guide all my life and here I was starting on a journey of doing so.

Arriving at camp, I walked through the front doors, and I was automatically greeted by Bill, Pat, and the rest of the crew.

"I've heard great things about you, it's a pleasure to finally meet the elk slayer," Ben, the owner, told me as he shook my hand. I settled into my room in the guide cabin and cracked open a beer with the guides. They filled me in on how operations work, and I felt at home.

Clients arrived the next day for their five-day hunt, and as they settled in, Bucky, another guide, and I headed out so I could learn the property. The style of hunting on Timber Bench Outfitters was that of sitting in ground blinds, for most of the property consists of thick scrub oak—impossible terrain to get in close to any wild animal. Meadows and water holes were scattered throughout the property, areas in which elk, deer, turkeys, bear, and moose fed and drank from. It was more of a waiting game style of hunt.

As the clients and guides mingled about, waiting for dinner, a client named Steve, who was hunting one of our drop camps, came into the lodge.

"Hey, Ben, I've got a deer tag and I'll pay one of your guides $500 if they can find me a nice buck!" Steve told Ben. Overhearing the conversation, I happened to look over just as Ben pointed right at me.

"There's your guide," he said to Steve.

With limited knowledge of the property, I focused on what I did know: the habitat for mule deer. At the bottom of the property, a series of rock cliffs and meadows scattered along the thick scrub oak. An old mining road ran through, creating vegetation for the mule deer. I had noticed this area when I drove through and thought to myself, *That looks like mule deer country*.

The guides and Ben made their suggestions as to where I should take Steve, because they wanted me to be successful, and pointed me in the right direction. I chose to sleep on it, deciding in the morning where Steve and I would hunt. I felt a need to prove myself—perhaps it was because I was the only female guide, or maybe I needed to prove something to myself.

Steve met me at camp the next morning and we drove down the road to the area I hadn't been able to stop thinking about. We parked the truck and walked the steep road in the dark. Once the sun brought daylight to the landscape, I realized we were way too low to see any animals. The vegetation was too tall to see anything. We needed to climb higher up the hillside in order to glass for any animals. The term glass or glassing is used by hunters describing looking for animals thought their binoculars or spotting scopes. On my end this was a rookie mistake, but Steve remained a good sport and followed along behind me as we bushwhacked our way up, crawling half the time. We wondered where all these deer were hiding, as tracks and deer scat littered the hillside.

"We need to get to the top so we can glass down into all of this," I told Steve.

"All right let's do it," Steve replied as his breaths came heavy and his chest went up and down. I was impressed with Steve's drive and ability to keep up, since he came from California.

We finally reached the ridgeline and spent some time glassing but came up empty-handed. We decided to have lunch and stick it out till one p.m., but if we didn't see anything, we'd continue working along the ridge, glassing down both sides.

Steve and I talked about life, and he asked question after question about who I was and how I got to where I was now. There was a connection I found with my clients during these quiet, unexcited moments in the field. These connections were far more important and fulfilling to me than that of filling a tag.

Finishing my lunch, I got up and told Steve I was going to go peak over the backside of the ridge and glass for a minute. Steve agreed and told me he'd investigate the other side. After just a few minutes, I had an idea and made my way over to where Steve was glassing when I saw him on one knee, his rifle up to his shoulder. A beautiful mule deer buck stood just sixty yards in front of Steve.

The sound of the rifle shot echoed across the canyon as the buck kicked his back legs up. Sometimes, we work so hard on these hunts, and just like that, it happens. One must always be ready because that window of opportunity can be quick and if you're not ready, you'll miss it.

"Nicely done!" I told Steve as we exchanged high-fives! I could hear the worry in Steve's voice as he told me the shot was quick and he was unsure of his hit. Finding the blood trail, it was clear this buck wouldn't last long, as big piles of dark red blood scattered the ground. We were confident and continued.

Pieces of guts hung from the thick scrub oak, telling us Steve had hit this buck in the guts. Looking up, I saw the buck slowly wobbling along the old mining road, its stomach ripped open, guts and blood falling out.

"Finish him off!" I urgently told him. "I don't want this buck to suffer anymore!"

The buck was walking away from us and there was no way Steve was going to be able to get a heart or lung shot on this buck.

"Texas heart shoot him!" I told Steve. A Texas heart shot is when the shooter takes a shot directly through the ass, the bullet going straight into the animal's vitals. This phrase came from novice hunters acting like cowboys in the woods, shooting without aiming or taking a risky shot. In this case, this was our only option to put this buck down and end its suffering.

With one shot through the ass, the buck fell dead in its tracks. Hunting wasn't like you see it on TV shows. It can be hard and sometimes we make bad shots—and trust me, it doesn't sit well with us. When shots like this happen, we do everything in our power to end the suffering, and in this case, a Texas heart shot did the trick.

There was no manual for hunting. Sometimes, despite how hard you trained and practiced shooting, you still make mistakes. We are human after all. Going through an experience like this with someone creates a bond that will never be lost. It's a moment in time that just the two of you share. The emotions, persistence, teamwork, camaraderie, it's one of the other main reasons why I guide.

Steve and I enjoyed a moment, taking photos and soaking it all in. The antlers on this buck consisted of kickers coming off each side, and scars riddled his face from past fights. He lived a long life, and now he would feed Steve and his family. Most of the Timber Bench Outfitters' property was accessible by four-wheelers or trucks, but there was no driving to this spot.

Once again throwing the pack on my shoulders, filled with wild, organic meat, we made our way down through the thick scrub oak, back to the trucks. We pulled into camp, windows down, with the music blasting as the buck sat atop Steve's truck for all the clients to see. Everyone hugged and high-fived, congratulating us on our success. Ben pulled me in for a big hug, a proud boss of his new eager employee trying to find her place.

"I knew you would get it done! That's why I choose you to guide him, Miss Tenacity," Ben told me.

My very first day on the job and not only did I prove my skill and place here at Timber Bench Outfitters, but a friendship was created. A friendship with Steve that still, five years later, continues to grow.

Early mornings, endless hours behind the binoculars, checking trail cameras, and heavy pack-outs unfolded in the following months. Growing up, for most of the hunts I was on, we would use the "bone-out" method in which we would cut the meat off the bone of the animal in the field, leaving the rest for the wild animals to feast on. At Timber Bench Outfitters, most of the animals killed were accessible by four-wheeler or a small pickup, allowing us to "gut" the animal and bring it back whole. Once back at the lodge, we would hang the elk (for example), skin it, butcher it, and place it into the big walk-in cooler.

It was an intimidating task knowing I would have to gut my first elk and I would have to do it with a client watching over my shoulder. I lost sleep over this, waiting for the day to come. The last thing I wanted to do was come across to my client like I didn't know what I was doing. So, I took every opportunity to go help when a client got an elk down, intently watching and asking questions as Bill quickly and smoothly gutted the elk. Soon, it was my turn, and as we drove up that bouncy road, I tried to maintain my cool. We took photos of the elk and celebrated its life, and then it was time to get to work. It felt as though I had gutted an elk many times before this, and I give thanks to the guides surrounding me who guided me through that experience.

Hunting can be an intimidating venture, and most people simply avoid it due to the rawness of it, and the challenges it brings. Many times, when I am out in the field hunting, I feel a deep connection with my ancestors and even the Native Americans, who relied on wild game to survive. Today's society has become so disconnected from not only our ancestors but where our food comes from. I understand it's not possible for all of us on this planet to be hunters, as there's only so much room in the wilderness and far from enough wild game to feed us all. But what we can do is bridge the gap between hunters and non-hunters: We can educate and tell our stories from the field. We can be honest about the mistakes and the hardships that come with it. We can tell stories as I do here about how it brought me confidence as a young girl and how it got me through the hardest times of my life. Hunting saved my life, and it can change yours too.

Let me tell you another hunting story. This five-day hunt took place in 2019 when I guided Brent and his father, Steve. Brent and Steve were all about hiking and putting an effort into notching their tag—my kind of hunters.

With a couple of inches of snow on the ground and nearly subzero temps, I knew exactly where we were going to hunt. Steve would sit in a ground blind called "the couch," while Brent and I would walk the logging roads, ever so slowly, hoping to sneak up on elk and get a shot. We dropped Steve off at his blind and continued across the snowy field toward the logging roads.

Shining my headlamp on the snowy ground, I could see elk tracks everywhere, and I knew they had been feeding in this field within the last couple of hours. The snow was crunchy, and we did our best to walk quietly. As we reached the entrance of the logging roads, I could hear the slightest sound of crunching coming from the thick aspen grove off to our right. I told Brent we needed to go down the road another hundred yards or so, so when these elk cross the road, they would walk right out on top of us.

Ever so slowly we made progress, and every time we stopped, I could hear them feeding. The morning was cold, and our cheeks were pink as we waited on the road, not moving, just listening. We could hear the leaves crunching but we couldn't see the elk, yet the sound was getting closer. I told Brent to get ready.

The lead cow walked out first, looking right at us. Our camouflage and stillness kept her from noticing us and she walked out across the road. The herd proceeded to follow her as several calves crossed, followed by their mothers. The cows and their calves crossed the road and we sat waiting patiently, hoping there was a bull following behind. Dark, tall tines revealed themselves, followed by a massive caramel-colored body. The bull was at eighty yards, perfectly broadside, and looking right at us.

"Take the shot!" I whispered to Brent. Raising his .300 mag to his shoulder, he leaned in and shot. A thwack echoed through the forest from Brent's shot, indicating the bullet hit its mark. Walking up to where the bull had stood, we were surprised to see shattered bone and blood spread out on the ground. Brent and I decided to follow the blood for a while and were confident as big blood spots brought color to the snowy ground. After a hundred yards, the blood stopped, and we decided to back out to grab reinforcements.

Grabbing Ben and a few guides we got back on the blood trail and found ourselves struggling to find a consistent trail. We spread out, our heads looking down at the ground. With every stretch between the blood becoming longer, my patience and positivity began to stretch thin. The bull never bedded down and was clearly moving just fine. We trailed him for nearly two thousand yards, and as we walked up on a meadow, we lost his tracks and couldn't pick up any more blood.

"I hate to say it, Brent, but I think this bull is going to live. It appears you hit him in the leg. He's going to survive, until the winter at least," I said, my heart heavy. I could see the emotion on their faces as they persisted to keep looking. I informed them it would be like finding a needle in a haystack, for they would have to try and find his tracks and blood trail again, and so I encouraged them to go sit by water. I could tell Brent felt terrible about the situation, and between the three of us, there was an unsaid gut-wrenching feeling.

Steve and Brent returned to camp after a few hours of sitting at a nearby water hole, turning up nothing.

"Draya, we would like to have a drink with you. Would you join us in our cabin here in a bit?" Steve asked me. We enjoyed some whiskey and drank to the elk gods. We reminisced on the memories of the past few days we had in the mountains, and they informed me they were done hunting. This was something I admired—it wasn't that common among hunters. The other clients in the camp tried to persuade Brent and Steve to continue hunting but Brent felt strongly that he had notched his tag, he just never got to keep the antlers and bring the meat home.

These are hard moments as a hunter, and as a guide, knowing an animal was injured, and it broke my heart thinking about this bull running around with only three legs. The wild holds no mercy and this bull most likely wouldn't make it through the winter. We were humbled by the experience and reminded that nothing in this life is ever guaranteed.

CHAPTER TWENTY-FIVE

As you've learned so far in this book, I have always been drawn to wild places, and when I received a message from my good friend Kevin, a.k.a. "Boulder," asking if I wanted to be his plus one on a Grand Canyon River trip, I wasted no time calling him to ask about details. Boulder informed me he and I would both be captains of a raft and that together we had more river experience than the entire rest of the group.

"Sign me up!" I responded. I was so excited about this opportunity.

"Draya, this trip is during September. Isn't that hunting season for you?" Boulder asked me.

"Yes, it is, but this is something I've always wanted to do, and there's no way I'm not going, so sign me up!" I told him.

The sixteen of us would spend fourteen days floating down the canyon, starting at Lees Ferry and ending at Diamond Creek, a total of 226 miles. We averaged eighteen miles a day, pushing a raft of nearly a thousand pounds through the wind, slow water, and rapids of varying sizes, from small ripples to monstrous hydraulic features and currents.

By now, I had five years of guiding experience under my belt and, in those years, had rowed thousands of river miles. I was confident in my skill, but butterflies fluttered in my stomach when I thought about rowing the biggest water I'd yet to see. I spent the summer leading up to the trip working full-time at Whitewater Rafting LLC, building up muscle and mental confidence. I wanted to be as strong as possible and to feel "one with the river" so when our time to push off at Lees Ferry came, I'd be ready.

I was looking forward to getting to know the others on the trip, as I only knew a couple of people on the roster prior to arriving. It was all part of the adventure. Boulder and I packed his car to the brim with gear and beer and headed south toward his aunt and uncle's place in Flagstaff, Arizona. We would meet everyone that night and go over what to expect on the trip. The next day we were shuttled to Lee's Ferry where we would rig the rafts, camp for the night, and push off the following morning.

The group consisted of folks of a variety of ages, and from all walks of life. We were required to sign a liability form after listening to the park ranger talk about the dangers we could face on the river. He told us a story about how someone once woke up one morning to a bat attached to their lip and how someone else was stung by a scorpion, resulting in being life-flighted out by helicopter. He reminded us how important safety was on the river, and that once we pushed off, we were on our own. There would be no walking out or quitting, so if we wanted to bail, this was the time to do so.

Later that night, as we sat around a fire, stories were shared from those who had rafted the canyon before, and in the dim light, I could see the excitement in everyone's eyes. I didn't sleep that night—the full moon brought light to everything it touched, and the anticipation of the adventure ahead had me far too energized for rest. Bats flew above our heads as they feasted on bugs, and Boulder would scream here and there, paranoid of the ranger's safety talk. Before I knew it, morning arrived, and it was time to rig the boats and push off onto what would be one of the most memorable adventures of my life.

Kevin, Olivia, Lexi, and I were assigned to a raft and quickly earned the title of "party barge." We were the youngest and bubbliest crew that was on the trip, and it didn't take us long to all become good friends. Lexi and Olivia were avid skiers, snowboarders, and mountain bikers. Neither of them had river experience but clearly lived a life of outdoor adventure and became the best bailers on the river.

The first few days consisted of slow flat water, giving us ample time to warm up our muscles and adapt to the insane power this river had. Leading up to this, the highest class rapid I had rowed was class IV. The depth of the Grand Canyon is such that it has its own classification of rapids, ranging from one to ten, while most rivers range from one to six.

Each morning my stomach would growl, but my appetite simply wasn't there as my nerves got the best of me. But as soon as we pushed off and my oars found their rhythmic pace, my nerves dissipated.

The power of the river was nothing like I had seen before. Amid the calm-looking water, an eddy line would catch the side of your raft and pull you out of the current. After several attempts, someone would finally free their raft from the eddy flowing back upriver and would then have to put even more effort into catching up with the crew again. This was something that happened to all of us, no matter how skilled we were. The power of the river was deceiving and humbling.

"Watch out for the helicopter eddy on the left side of this rapid," one of the captains would mention as we entered a rapid. A helicopter eddy is where the water essentially creates a whirlpool on the side of the river, which can be incredibly difficult to get out of.

One afternoon, I was in a raft with some ladies and we found ourselves getting sucked into a helicopter eddy.

I yelled at the girls, "Watch your oars and get ready to high side!" as we got tossed around, the side of our raft slamming into a massive rock and nearly flipping over sideways. Our raft managed to get sucked back into the current as we all looked at each other in shock that we didn't flip.

"Good teamwork, girls," I reassured them as a sigh of relief came over each one of us.

For this type of river trip to run smoothly, it required everyone to do their part in a cycle of duties such as cooking, washing dishes, and setting up and taking down the toilet, a.k.a. "the groover." On the fourth day of the rotation, you got a day off to enjoy yourself chore-free. As you cooked dinner or washed dishes together, it made for a great opportunity to get to know each other and bond, and ultimately, it helped everything run smoothly.

On the Grand Canyon, there is a leave-no-trace-behind policy, resulting in having to literally raft the shit and trash downriver. Each night we would pull into a campsite, all of them different and unique in their own way. One night, we passed around a vape pen and had the most competitive bocce ball game I've ever been a part of, all while trying not to touch the big white flowers (sacred datura), for if we did, we would end up in a painful, and eventually lethal, hallucinogenic trance.

The sky held smoke from a wildfire above and we wondered what was happening to the earth we couldn't see from the bottom of the vast canyon.

One morning, Anthony, one of the fellow adventures on the trip, came running through the campground with his guitar in hand, clearly on a mission. A few minutes later, he and his girlfriend, appeared, a diamond ring on her finger! Anthony was, and is, a musician, so many evenings were spent sitting in a circle as Anthony serenaded us with his musical poetry. While on the river, Anthony began working on a song about our trip through the canyon and every night would play back what he had created so far. We were blown away by his talent and honored to be included in such a beautiful piece of art.

With a couple of days on the river, everyone seemed to be getting along just fine. Reaching mile 44: President Harding Rock Camp, We got our camp set up, and for those of us who weren't on kitchen duty, we pulled out bocce ball and libations. Later that night, we sat in a circle playing a game of Slap the Bag. For those of you who don't know this game, it's very simple: You start with a bag of wine and must ask someone a question; in return they answer, slap the bag of wine, take a healthy swig, and then must ask someone else a different question. It makes for an easy way to get to know each other.

Oliva was up to bat, and she asked me, "Draya, what is the scariest thing that has happened to you?"

Being completely honest and vulnerable, I responded with, "My brother sexually abused me when I was young." The crew went silent, not knowing how to react to such a response, something I had witnessed time and time again. The topic got brushed off, as this wasn't the time and place to explain my trauma, and so I kept the game going, asking someone else a question. Soon dinner was ready, and people started to move off toward the kitchen to grab a plate of food.

"Draya, hey, I want to talk to you about your answer from earlier in the game," one of my friends said to me as he pulled a chair up, sitting down next to me. We spent a good while exchanging stories from our traumatic past, and it felt good knowing someone was able to relate. It felt good to talk about it with someone who understood the pain, anger, forgiveness, and the process of trying to heal. The magic that comes from telling and owning your truth can be a powerful tool in the healing process. Not only does this allow healing for yourself but being vulnerable gives others the strength to own theirs too.

Day seven arrived and we stopped at Phantom Ranch where we would make a switch—some people only signed up for seven days. A few of our friends left, and a few new ones came in, changing the dynamic of the trip for the second half. The hike from the top of the canyon to the river was roughly ten miles, so we had some time to kill. Oliva and I went into the gift shop to purchase trinkets and send out postcards to friends and loved ones. We enjoyed a beer, and the atmosphere was a lovely change but was almost foreign after being disconnected from the real world for a week. We made our way back to the rafts so we could continue down the canyon to finish off the second week of our trip. Pushing off from the bank, my heart skipped a beat, as this was when the bigger rapids would come into play.

At mile 52.4, we reached Nankoweap Creek where we hiked up to the ancestral Puebloan granaries. Nearly one thousand years ago, ancestral Puebloans hauled their grain, including pumpkin seeds and corn, from the river delta below and used square windows cut into the sandstone as storage units. The granary helped keep the food dry during floods and protected it against rodents and other hungry critters.

We took the trail up the steep canyon and sat among them, feeling the energy of the people who once lived there. The view was like nothing I'd seen before; I felt like I was living in a dream.

At mile 61.7, we hiked up the Little Colorado River. The water was so blue and beautiful. Small waterfalls and channels held just enough water for us to float down with our life jackets on as we laid on our backs, our feet first, giggling like little kids. It reminded me of my younger days when we would play at the creek for hours, the river becoming our playground. I looked around at the adults, smiles filling everyone's faces. Jumping back in, we created a floating train, holding onto the life jacket of the person in front, meandering down the channels, playing to our hearts' desire. There was no one else around for miles and as I looked up the tall canyon wall, I felt small, just a dot on this planet and so incredibly lucky to experience such a magical place.

Most days I would intently watch and follow Phil's line as he (in my opinion) was the most skilled guide on that trip. He was so confident in reading the water and always favored the conservative line when going down the rapids. I watched how he pointed his raft and let the water do the work for him. After a three-mile stretch of "read and run" rapids ranging from class III to V, we pulled into Granite Rapids Campground. We arrived early and had an afternoon of exploring the desert canyon behind camp.

The sound of Granite Rapid was loud in the background, as we were camped just a few hundred yards upriver from it. While walking along a trail created by those who have walked this canyon before me, I stumbled upon a set of dragonfly wings laying on the canyon floor. I took this as an omen that everything would be okay as we proceeded on the second half of this trip.

Mile 93.9. I didn't sleep that night, just like most, as the rapids howled and crashed, echoing off the canyon walls. My nerves got the best of me, and I used the toilet a few times that morning knowing this would be the biggest rapid yet. Granite Rapid is a class VIII, made up of a cliff on the right side of the river and a boulder field on the left side, creating only one path for the raft to get through. Big lateral waves came off the wall, forcing you to point your raft at the cliff, teeing up each wave so it wouldn't flip you. If you didn't tee-up the waves, meaning hitting them square on the front of the raft, you would most likely flip sideways as the waves crashed into the side of the boat. The water was so powerful that there was no way of crashing into the cliff wall, and so powerful that you had to use every bit of muscle power to lean into your rowing, pushing strong through the waves as it drenched the two people in the front of the raft.

It was exhilarating! As I crashed through the first wave, my body went to work as I leaned into my oars. Being so small, I needed to utilize my body in a way so I wouldn't get tossed out, bracing one foot in front of me and one in back. Each time we crashed through a wave, I would holler at the girls, "Lean in, lean in!" With their combined weight in the front, it helped keep the front of the raft from lifting too far up. The wild wet ride only lasted for a matter of seconds and then it was time to get to work bailing water so we wouldn't get sucked in the helicopter eddy just below the rapid on the right. Hooting and hollering, the three of us were filled with adrenaline and life, humbled by the river and the magnificent canyon it flowed through.

With each rapid, my confidence grew but knowing the sheer power of the river, I never fully trusted it. In my previous experience, the second I got cocky was the moment my raft would flip. Since our trip was only fourteen days long, we were limited on time to explore the slot canyons and waterfalls while pushing high-mileage days on the water. Most river trips are twenty-plus days, allowing full days to relax and explore, so we took advantage of the shorter hikes and would briefly experience their magic and glory before having to get back on the river and continue on.

At one point on the trip, the river narrowed down to just seventy-six feet wide and eighty-five feet deep. The rock in the canyon during this narrow stretch is called Vishnu Schist. "The Vishnu complex is schist, gneiss, and granite. The Vishnu mountains resulted from plate tectonic collision of ocean floor sediments and basalts with the North American continent. Under great pressure and heat, sedimentary and igneous rocks metamorphosed to form the black and silver mica-schist of the Vishnu. White or pink granite plutons, dikes, and sills intruded the schist. After metamorphism, some granites became gneiss, a rock that looks like granite with wavy layering" (grandcanyonnaturalhistory.com). The water flowed calmly but quickly through this section, and I looked up in awe at the storyline on the wall in front of me.

The next series of big rapids we would crush through were Hermit (VIII), Crystal (VIII), Bedrock (VII), Upset (VIII), and the famous Lava Falls (IX). These are the bigger rapids of roughly eighty total rapids. While we were scouting Upset, a helicopter flew just overhead of us. We waved them off and questioned what happened. We came to find out someone had a heart attack on the river and needed to be life-flighted out. The only way to get out of the canyon is either floating down to the takeout, which takes days, or by helicopter.

The management of permits on the canyon is spread out, that way everyone has campgrounds to themselves, and when you're on the river it feels as though you're the only ones down there. My body was becoming strong as there were no days off from rowing, besides a few minutes here and there to take a break. Despite how much I drank and ate, I still managed to go home weighing less than when we started on the journey.

The phrase often spoken on this trip was "You're always above Lava." Lava is the biggest of all the rapids on the canyon and it just so happened to be toward the end of our trip. It was as if the entire trip we were preparing ourselves for the massive, roaring rapid, and when the day came, I was ready.

We took a slow morning getting out of camp, allowing the

water levels to rise back up, that way, come afternoon when we had to face Lava, we had a little more water to work with. Water releases are done every day on the Grand, making the water levels ebb and flow.

We pulled over just above Lava and made our way along the trail tucked into a boulder field. Looking down at the crashing water, butterflies filled my stomach. A giant hole, named "the ledge hole," makes up the entrance of the rapid, white water rising and smashing back into the giant hole. The line was to follow the bubble line that floated down into the rapid, the tip of your raft nearly touching the right side of the hole.

Brian and I somehow pushed off at the same time, and it was a race to see who got to the entrance first. I pushed with all I had, knowing I needed to set up correctly, otherwise, the one-thousand-pound bucket boat would soon be upside down, pinned on some rock. I entered the top of Lava. The power of the river naturally pushed us right, and if we didn't have the right placement, we would get pushed right into the "cheese grater" rock. I was in charge of rowing the raft that was filled with the shit from the groover, and as I entered the entrance of the rapid, I was calm. All the nerves I had experienced on this trip were gone.

Halfway down we crashed through the v-wave, my riders leaning into the massive wave as I leaned in and pushed through. We were clear of the cheese grater rock and only had a few smaller rapids left to go through. Arms and fists pounded the air as excitement and relief that we made it safely through came over us! Turning the raft around we set up safely just in case the rafts following had swimmers or any carnage. Every raft made it through safely, and as we pulled over onto Margarita Beach we partied like it was 1999.

Back in the rafts, the wind blew upriver with vengeance, and we all were struggling to keep the rafts from going downriver. If you weren't constantly working on keeping your raft in the current, the wind would push you into an eddy in which you would end up upriver, fighting to get back into the current. We were all exhausted and thirsty, for there was no way to drink and row the raft at the same time. As we came around a bend, all our rafts got pushed into a giant eddy, and for a good hour we fought the battle. Sara and I worked together—I would push and she would pull at the same time—and inch by inch we made progress. We decided to pull over for the day, the unclaimed campground was now called "fuck you beach."

The wind showed no signs of slowing down; hoodies, hats, and buffs were pulled out as the younger ones gathered in a raft, enjoying each other's company. Meanwhile, the older ones gathered down by the river sipping on bourbon they refused to share. Makings for deli sandwiches were pulled for dinner, and all duties for the evening were disregarded.

The next morning made for a quick clean-up and push-off, for we had miles to make up from the windy day yesterday. The wind was far from gone but we pushed on.

The next couple of days were filled with slow water and meaningful conversations. We realized that our time here on the canyon would soon be over and we would return to the real world. None of us were particularly excited about that. The days had gone by far too fast, and we relished the final moments we had left.

Finally, it was our last night in the canyon. We all gathered in a circle, our cups filled up with the good stuff. Anthony pulled out his guitar and, with anticipation, we became silent waiting to hear the masterpiece of "Whistlin' Down the Water." Tears rolled down our cheeks as Anthony sang about our adventures and the beauty of the canyon we were so lucky to experience the past thirteen days.

WHISTLIN' DOWN THE WATER
BY ANTHONY RUPTAK

I'm a-floatin' in the Grand Canyon, heron and sandstone.
Without a single care — well, we've found ourselves a hole.
Just a-pissin' in the water, maybe we are dead after all.
A cloudy head of spines, a blade of Vishnu spire, a heart of granite doom.

O-oo oo oo oo, whistlin' down the water. (x2)

I'm a-ridin' in a rubber ducky with my camera and my PFD.
Just a-punchin' through the sick-nasty, got a picture at the granary.
I think this year will be the one that goes down in history.
A complicated mind, eroding over time, the womb of the Hopi (and we wonder why we just don't stay here).

O-oo oo oo oo, whistlin' down the water. (x2)

I'm a-watchin' how the sun shines against the tectonic sheets.
She's a-wounded by a long life, but sturdy in her seams.
I'm a-broken by a bystander; hooved and humble, she's a waste lander.
A smoky liquid sky, alujah adoni, pure again in your tether.

O-oo oo oo oo, whistlin' down the water.
O-oo oo oo oo, the great forgiver and forgetter.

I'm a-wakin' by the moon, shearing by the sail of an empty stream.
Bound in flight and set on re-sealin' all our cracks and dreams and leaks.
I wonder always of our great failure to withhold our reverence for our claim-stakers.
We're always asking why, Detura valentine, a rowdy lot of risk-takers.

O-oo oo oo oo, whistlin' down the water. (x2)

I've been working on perfection, baptisms always come in threes.
A holy-water blood transfusion from the well of ancient you and me.
I'm a-listenin' to the busy chatter of the ring-tailed bandits and
the song of Saturn.
We're deafened by our plight, ignoring warning signs, the siren
on the sea, singin'.

O-oo oo oo oo, whistlin' down the water. (x2)

I smell the burning of a forest fire from the world up above the rim.
It's a-blockin' out the stars, carried on the passage of the wind.
The whirlybird is looking for survivors, maybe last night's
lightning was the big red button.
A selfish little life, a spotty alibi, forgotten how to be human.

O-oo oo oo oo, whistlin' down the water.
O-oo oo oo oo, I miss the latter of the former.

I've been turning on a dime and you are throwing in a rope.
Worry slowing to a grind, heartache turning into black-hills gold.
Travelin' through time, reaching through the cosmic telephone.
Tiptoe through the crypto, Little Colorado, polished shale and bone.
(The lava knows we're never really through it.)

O-oo oo oo oo, whistlin' down the water.
O-oo oo oo oo, the echo of the seekers.
O-oo oo oo oo, just a-screamin' toward the future.
O-oo oo oo oo, whistlin' down the water.

CHAPTER TWENTY-SIX

During my mid- to late-twenties, I spent most of my time alone, hiking, scouting for hunting season, training for races, shed hunting, or going for long dirt-road drives. I built up the back of my pickup with the help of some raft-guide buddies and spent three springs and summers sleeping wherever I chose to park that night. Having a home on wheels gave me freedom and simplified the things I owned. I had no interest in dating at this time because I was on a self-love/growth/discovery adventure.

One summer I decided to sign up for a train-to-hunt race. To train, I spent every morning doing yoga, then guide two trips on the river and get in a workout that evening. I stopped drinking and became conscious of the food I was putting into my body. I got down to a lean 118 pounds, and my mind became the clearest it ever had been. This race consisted of high-intensity workouts while shooting your bow in between the moves, simulating an elevated heart rate while hunting. After completing the workout portion, the ladies threw in sixty pounds while the guys threw one hundred pounds into their packs, and we raced up to the summit of Powderhorn Ski Hill. The quicker you got to the top, the less amount of time was added to your final score.

The first half of the hike went swimmingly as I made progress, but the second half was a living hell. As I struggled to put one foot in front of the other, I listened to Carrie Underwood's song, "The Champion," the same one I listened to on repeat while running the half marathon a couple of years back. The confidence I had found over the years of exploration was holding strong as I pushed myself to keep climbing the mountain. This was a metaphor for life at the time and I embraced the message it held.

Crossing the finish line at nearly 10,500 feet, I was filled with pride for the dedication I had put into preparing for this. Hiking that mountain was physically one of the hardest things I had done. As I rode the ski lift down to the resort, the vastness of western Colorado presented itself in all her glory. The best playground and teacher there is. The contestants and supporters gathered in the restaurant as the winners were announced. I felt good about my performance but not about my shooting score from the 3-D portion. Hearing my name on the speakers, I was overjoyed because I got third place. I had worked so hard and in the end it paid off. As I stood on the podium holding my medal, I felt a new level of confidence and I got a glimpse of the woman I was becoming.

I want to take a moment and thank those of you who welcomed me into your homes, giving me a bedroom to occupy during my time of self-discovery and healing. I tried to live with "friends" but ended up hating it and moved out as soon as I could. They would party all night, leaving a mess of pizza boxes and empty champagne bottles, yet I was the bad roommate for leaving my dishes in the sink. I would head out for a hike while they would be lounging on the couch with their friends, already drunk, and would make comments on how I was "always going outside," or "for a run." I'd like to think these comments came from a place of insecurities in these roommates and not because they thought going outside "too much" was a thing.

The more time I spent alone, the more of it I craved. The friendships with those in the Roaring Fork Valley I had found seemed to fade away and I was no longer enticed to go spend money at the loud bar or party late into the night. I found the solitude among the aspen groves intoxicating as I got lost in the way the branches danced above and the breeze it brought to my face.

During the summer, I took advantage of any free time I could to get out and scout for wild game. All I could think about was hunting season and putting miles on my boots. I daydreamed of a life someday where I would be able to financially sustain myself through the hunting industry. In 2019, I spent a quiet and cold winter living in Marble, Colorado, population fifty-two. The cozy cabin was thirty-by-thirty feet, just big enough to fit my friend Dylan and me. My bedroom was that of a closet in which I hung a shower curtain for my door.

There was no Wi-Fi, TV, or cell service in the cabin tucked away in the big mountains. I dreaded the drive back into town because my phone would blow up with texts, missed calls, and endless emails. Dylan and I spent hours doing puzzles or talking, and on Christmas Day, we hiked ten miles, all the while Dylan told me stories of his days as a hunting guide, his fingers pointing to this mountain and that mountain.

No matter the time or day, we talked about our dreams and what we wanted in life. We were both seeking the quiet of mountain living and found a deep connection within ourselves. I was so caught up in my own journey that I didn't realize Dylan was going through the same thing. Most of my childhood and teenage years were spent being the center of attention, and I thrived off that. Now as I was focusing on my healing journey, I traded that in for the solitude of the mountains, the peace and quiet.

The summer flew by as I worked as a raft guide and spent all the time I could out scouting for hunting season. I had become obsessed with learning about big game, especially elk. It was all I could think about, and honestly, to this day, that's still true.

Having just finished my second trip on the river for the day, I raced out to the nearby national forest because I wanted to sit at a water hole for the evening to see what game was using it. There were only a few hours of daylight left so naturally I was in a hurry to get out to this spot. I had a couple of miles of easy trail to walk before I came to the water hole so I decided to go in light. I grabbed my bear spray and headed out. I remember thinking to myself as I left the truck behind me that the more time I spent in the mountains, the higher the chance of something happening was. The thought passed through quickly as new thoughts came in about what I would see later that night.

As I came upon a meadow, I thought to myself, *Draya, you should stop and glass this meadow quickly, just to make sure you don't spook anything from it.* But being in such a hurry, I ignored the thought and kept walking. About halfway through the meadow, I heard sticks breaking not too far off. Looking up, I saw a bear cub climbing the tree and the mama bear standing on the back legs next to it, her nose in the air and her ears pinned back.

I stopped dead in my tracks, and I knew they had seen me long before I saw them. I slowly started to back off, getting my bear spray ready just in case mama was about to charge. I had many run-ins with bears over the years; the majority of the time, they were running away, but not this time. Mama wasn't too sure about my presence and barked at me. Daylight was starting to fade and the last thing I wanted was for the sow to be circling me, so I kept slowly moving back on the trail.

She dropped down onto all fours and started to circle the meadow. She was wanting to get downwind of me and get my scent. All I could think about at this moment was, *Do not die, do not let this bear kill you.*

I started to run, looking back every other step to keep my eyes on her. I could see her slowly working around the meadow toward me, and just as I turned back to look at her, my foot found a small rock, then my ankle cracked and rolled to the side. I dropped to the ground in immense pain, and I could feel my ankle begin to swell in my boot.

Great, now I was on the ground, and mama bear would be on top of me any second. I wasn't ready to die, and visions of the sow tearing me to pieces got me up off the ground. With my bear spray out and ready, I slowly rose above the tall ground foliage, but to my surprise, the sow was nowhere to be seen. I had heard many stories of bear attacks where the sow would come back for round two, three, and even four to make sure the threat was gone.

I started to limp back to the truck, finding a stick to help with my throbbing ankle, constantly watching my back in hopes she wasn't following me. After what felt like an eternity, I made it back to the truck just as it was getting dark, and relief came over me, thankful that I wasn't dinner for the sow and her cub. A lesson was learned the hard way as I drove back to society, my ankle throbbing inside my boot.

CHAPTER TWENTY-SEVEN

Growing up, the ocean always had its way of drawing me in, mesmerizing me with its hum created from constant, crashing waves and the way the air felt on my skin. After moving to Colorado, I started missing the rainforest, its smell, and the sounds of the many birds singing their songs. I missed the feel of the sand under my toes, the moist air on my skin, and walking among the tall evergreens swaying above me. I had made great progress in my healing journey thus far, and I started feeling a pull from the West Coast to go visit those places from my childhood, places of horror and of grounding and adventure.

I lost my job as a preschool teacher's assistant due to COVID-19, then I ended up with a yellow lab born from my parent's dog Ginger. I figured there was no better time than now to go back to my old stomping grounds and reconnect with my younger self. With Remi, my three-month-old puppy, in my back seat and a soul-seeking desire for healing, we drove west toward the golden sun that set over the ocean's horizon.

Our first stop was Klickitat, Washington, where I would hunt for deer growing up (I shared a story previously in the book about this special place). To start the trip out, I wanted to soak in the energy these mountains held. I pulled into the familiar gravel lot and pitched a tent down by the river, the same spot I had slept at many times growing up.

The weather was typical, rainy and gray, but that didn't stop Remi and I from exploring. We played by the river and built up a firepit for that night's fire. Hunting here as a young girl instilled confidence and an appreciation for hard work as I followed my dad up these steep hills in search of the black-tailed deer. I wanted to reconnect with that young girl I used to be, and so I laced up my boots and headed to the trailhead just up the road.

The landscape and the smell of the oak trees were all so familiar as we made quick work hiking along the trail. Memories came flooding back of early mornings and heavy pack-outs. When Remi and I got back to camp, I looked at her and noticed her body was covered in ticks. I had completely forgotten this area was prone to ticks, especially in the spring! I frantically picked each one off her yellow coat as she wiggled to free herself. As I threw them out of the tent I realized we needed to leave or this fight to keep the ticks off of us would continue. Checking myself, I, too, had several crawling up my arms and I shivered in disgust at the creepy insects.

Pulling up to my friend's house, it felt good to see the girlfriends whom I grew up with. A warm energy welcomed me into their home, and they let me know I could stay for however long I needed. During this trip, I had full intentions of focusing my attention on the emotions and the sensations that would come to my body as I relived my childhood playground, letting that help me heal.

The house I grew up in was now owned by people I didn't know, and as I knocked on their front door, the memories were already flooding in. A kind, red-haired woman opened the door with a big smile on her face. I introduced myself and told her this was the home I grew up in, that I was working on writing a book, and I asked if I could explore the property a bit. She encouraged me to enjoy the land for however long I needed and to come and go as I pleased.

Grabbing a notebook and my camera from the truck, Remi and I headed to the pond that Mom and Dad had built, an icon of our property. The flowers were dead, and there was tall brown grass everywhere. The waterfalls were dry and covered in dead maple leaves. Algae and brown soupy water filled the bottom of the ponds as rain fell softly from the sky. This had been a place enjoyed by many growing up, bright flowers filling the rock beds and bees buzzing about in search of nectar. The energy was still there, and despite the dead foliage and overall lack of upkeep, I could still feel it. Memories from nighttime skinny-dipping and endless hours of swimming under the warm summer sun brought a smile to my face, and tears to my cheeks. Life was simple then as our days were filled with outdoor adventure.

A dark, low-hanging cloud brought heavy rain and I ran toward what used to be Tinker's horse stall to seek shelter. The rain hammered loud on the aluminum roof and Remi was fully entertained by the chickens that were cooped in. This had been a place of escape as a young girl. Hours were spent brushing and talking with Tinker, for his energy had a way of calming my mind. A smile covered my face as I relived those moments that had brought me peace as a young girl.

Soon, the rain was done falling from the sky and I ventured out toward the far end of the property where I had shot my first deer and elk. Pine needles held the grass at bay and opened the forest floor as the trees had gotten taller and were now blocking out any sunlight. The old wooden swing set we had placed in the corner of the field many years back to use as a deer blind had now fallen over and was starting to rot.

As I walked through the maze of trees, I saw something purple on the ground just ahead. Walking up I noticed a shotgun shell laying on the ground. Picking it up, I soon realized it was from Dad's sweet sixteen-gauge shotgun, the gun I had used to kill my very first buck. Chills rushed through my body at this moment that told me I was right where I was supposed to be. I took some time to embrace this unplanned discovery, and while doing so, I noticed there were no other ferns close by, except the small bundle next to where the shotgun was just lying. The death of the small buck I had killed that day had brought new life to the earth.

It was time to move on and I let my feet naturally take the course. I wandered aimlessly through more fir trees, the smell of dirt and pine needles filling my senses, just like I remembered it as a kid.

My feet suddenly stopped, and my heart picked up its pace. Taking a deep breath, I looked at the ground before me, now a blanket of weeds covering up the dirty secrets of what had happened here in the past. Years ago, there was a cabin that my brothers had built, tucked away, hiding among the trees—the place my brother had raped me. Tears washed down my face, and I let them flow. A sting of pain coursed through my abdomen as I relived the searing pain of my brother forcing his dick into me from behind.

I stayed in this spot for a long while, hoping I could remember the details of what happened after my brother was done. My memory had become blurry of this, I'm sure due to my strong will to survive the trauma. I couldn't get these details to resurface, and the emotional roller coaster began. I could feel the fear I felt then, trapped by the unknown of what would happen if I ran or if I told someone. The anger toward my brother boiled hot under my skin as a flash of heat came over my body.

I wanted to reach out and hug the younger me and encourage her to own her truth, to speak it loudly and scream it from the tops of mountains. I wanted to tell her to be courageous, that she was worthy of love and confidence. I wanted to take her hand and bring her to a sunny warm place of love and safety and let her cry in my arms. All these things clearly weren't possible, but I realized I could apply this to myself now. I would scream my truth from the tops of the mountains, and I would let the tears flow freely as if someone was there holding me.

Most of my healing had been done alone, as I've mentioned previously how the tunnel vision of my family created a wall between us. I had expected to feel more emotion toward my brother and the memory of him violating me, but I was pleasantly surprised with how my mind handled revisiting this place. I felt a wave of empowerment to continue paving my way through healing and self-discovery. To own my truth and to let my story bring hope to others so they, too, can leave the demons behind. Closing my eyes and lifting my head to the sky, I breathed out through my mouth, releasing my vibrations of love. By doing so, I would release the trap in which my young self had been stuck and give her the freedom to heal.

I took the old gravel road we walked many times as kids up and over the hill to the pond. The blackberry bushes were overgrown, creating a tunnel for most parts of the trail. I knew the exact spot I was going to, for I had gone there many times as a girl. In the distance, I could hear the frogs as the crickets echoed off the water into the spring air.

Following a game trail that veered off the road, I tried to find the spot I sat at many times, but everything had become overgrown. Mossy branches hung low from the trees as water from the rain dripped from them. I jumped back on the road and followed it till I reached the pond. The old tire swing had broken in half and lime-green moss dangled from the end of it. The firepit next to the water's edge was now overgrown, and it seemed odd that those who lived close by didn't utilize this space. Not much had changed—it was still a lush paradise—and as I looked out, a beaver peeked his head from below the surface, dove back down, then reappeared somewhere else.

Returning to these places from my childhood started to connect the dots of how I had survived. I was able to appreciate each place for its ability to bring me peace and grounding when I needed it the most. My mind back then was a constant battle zone and if it wasn't for these places, who knows if I would have survived. I'm incredibly grateful for these wild places—without them, life would have been too hard.

As I explored the overgrown countryside, there was a constant tale being told. These places I used to visit held their purpose during those years as I lived in the fight-or-flight mentality. Having moved on and healed drastically, I didn't need to sit near these wild places anymore. And as the foliage grew more and more, it held back the old version of me, keeping her safe under the many layers of moss and ferns. It was time to leave her in the past, to let her go, to be free, and to let her be as she always dreamed. She now was one with the wild. It was time to harness the woman I always dreamed of becoming. It was time to move on.

CHAPTER TWENTY-EIGHT

I was redefining who I was, and in that process, I started feeling quite lonely. The people I had called friends now seemed like strangers, or perhaps I wasn't into partying anymore, and I longed to find like-minded individuals to connect with. I decided to move to Steamboat Springs, Colorado, hoping the western town would bring a healthier social life. I got a job with a very wealthy family as their housekeeper and nanny and connected with the kids instantly.

But the ugly and detailed nightmares had returned, which left me feeling sick to my stomach and unable to leave the house as tears rolled down my cheeks. *Would these horrific memories haunt me for the entirety of my life?* I pondered. Feeling vulnerable, I posted on social media regarding my situation, and in response, a girl reached out to me suggesting I look into EMDR therapy. EMDR stands for "Eye Movement Desensitization and Reprocessing," a form of therapy to help you process the negative images, emotions, beliefs, and body sensations associated with traumatic memories that seem to be stuck. These can contribute to a range of mental health problems.

I had previously read about this type of therapy in the book, *The Body Keeps the Score* by Bessel van der Kolk. Kolk, a psychiatrist, researcher, and therapist, breaks down these five topics: the rediscovery of trauma, "this is your brain on trauma," the minds of children, the imprint of trauma, and the paths to recovery." So, when I was referred to an EMDR therapist, I had no doubts that this form of therapy was exactly what I needed to keep progressing in my healing.

As Ashley and I worked together, I came to realize I was holding myself back, for the many years of feeling unworthy was still ingrained in my body. I held a lot of anger toward my brother and my body ached for forgiveness but my idea of that was clouded by the old teachings of the LLC. I simply could not bring myself to forgive and forget something that took away my innocence, which led to tapping into the young, sweet, innocent, and carefree girl I was before I was sexually abused. I decided to focus on her, to harness her love and energy and apply it to everything I did.

With each session, I would cross my arms over my chest or hold them down, resting my hands on my thighs, and as I breathed in deep, I would tap back and forth, and there in those calm moments, memories of her would come back to me. Toward the end of each session, I would stow away my negative thoughts and emotions someplace they were locked away but in a space I could revisit them. I chose a rubber tote with buckles to keep the lid secure. Then at the end of each session, I would visit a place that made me feel calm and grounded. I chose an aspen grove in the summertime, and there I would lay on my back feeling the warm sunshine and cool breeze on my face as the leaves danced about above me.

We dove back into that rubber tote each session, and as I breathed and connected with my body, it would tell me what parts of me needed healing. Through this form of therapy, I was able to let go of the resentment and shame I was still holding onto, I was able to learn how to forgive on my own terms and forgive myself, but most importantly, I was able to reconnect with the girl I once was. Standing there on the old gravel road above the cabin my brother had raped me in, I reached my hand out to the scared and wounded teenager. Grasping on tight to my younger self, I led her away to someplace safe, an old cabin tucked away in the rain forest. There she gave my wounded self the love and protection I never received after my abuse.

When I opened my eyes, coming back to reality hit me: I have the power within myself to move past this, to no longer be controlled by my trauma, to trust in that young, carefree girl because she lived a life free of pain, fear, and resentment. She loved unconditionally, ran barefoot in the grass—she was free then, and she is again free now.

CHAPTER TWENTY-NINE

Living in Steamboat Springs, I was able to connect with the women of Rocky Mountain Sportswomen, a nonprofit organization with the goal of bringing women together by hosting free events, such as ice fishing, snowshoe hiking, and waterfowl seminars. I finally was finding women who shared common interests, something that had been lacking my entire life.

Through my connections with RMSW, I was invited over to Bevan's house to try on a women-specific hunting and outdoor clothing brand called Ridge Patrol. Bevan didn't have much experience with hunting, just the small amount of turkey and waterfowl hunting she went on with her boyfriend at the time. She felt unflattering and embarrassed in her hunting clothes and would change at the truck after the hunt, not wanting to be seen in public. She decided to start a brand of clothing that would not only look good on women but also perform just as well. Knocking on her front door, I was eager to see the clothes and had a feeling this would turn into something bigger.

A hopeful feeling brought butterflies to my stomach as I waited on her front doorstep. Bevan welcomed me into her home with a big smile and we wasted no time getting to know one another. As I tried on the clothes, I was very happy with what she had but I had a few ideas on how she could make them better. I offered to test out the clothing on an upcoming Arizona deer hunt and even offered to get some photos for her social media. A business partnership with Bevan was evolving, I just didn't know it yet.

As the months went on, I became more involved in helping Bevan create the first line of Ridge Patrol and soon she offered me the position as the cofounder. I was ecstatic! Ever since I was a young girl, I knew I wanted to work in the hunting industry and here and now the opportunity lay in front of me. I was beyond thrilled to create clothes for women that would bring them confidence in the field and to take my stand in the male-dominated industry.

I spent the summer testing out our first line of Ridge Patrol clothing, spending countless hours exploring and looking for big game. Starting out as a small business with no credibility isn't easy and I knew I needed to pour my heart, soul, and time into this brand in order to gain traction. Our following began to grow, and our presale orders were coming in! August arrived and our clothes were finally in women's hands. As soon as I stopped working full-time at my other jobs and started putting my time and attention into Ridge Patrol, the anxiety faded and we started to see progress. Summer turned to fall and archery season was here. It was time to really put the clothing and myself to the test.

Those of you who hunt archery understand that many factors must come together to have a successful harvest. Wind, thermals, scent, a clear shot for the arrow to make a lethal shot, gear functionality, weather, you name it—they are all elements that are out of your control, but sometimes it all comes together and luck finds you.

It was the last hour of light and we were hunting our way back to camp after a big day on the mountain and failed opportunities to get in close for a shot. We were on day seven of hunting, waking at 4:30 every day and not getting to sleep until ten p.m., and nearly fifty miles under our belt. Naturally, I fell behind when hiking with others as I stand at 5'1", and on this day in particular, it was eating away at me. I started to talk negatively to myself, mumbling, "You're not strong enough," focusing on the pain that was coursing through my muscles and not the strength within them. My heart raced as I tried to take deep breaths. Unable to do so, I fell to the ground and wept. Salty tears drenched my face and binocular harness as I released every ounce of doubt, pain, fear, resentment, and negativity. I screamed as my hands fell to the earth, grabbing onto the grassy shrubs. Soon my heart slowed and I became grounded. Later that night as I sat around the fire, I wrote this:

> *I thought about quitting today. I thought about hanging up my bow for good. And just as the thought came to me, it felt as though I was punched in the gut, and down I went, falling to the earth. Through blurry eyes, I looked up at the mountain glowing pink in the setting sun, and I asked myself, "When have you ever given up because something was hard?" As I wept, I gasped in the clarity of the mountain air. Visions of my younger self came flooding through my memory. A young girl who ran to the forest to hunt any chance she could get, a girl who found confidence bit by bit in the rain forest. She never gave up, and she won't now. The rugged mountains and the elk that thrive here, they have things to teach me, and today I was their student.*

My partner at the time and I got to know each other very well after spending nearly a month in the elk woods. You learn a lot about a person when you experience the highs and lows of hunting. It brings out your true colors. Hunting for me has always been an emotional sport, for I have such high expectations of myself, yet at the same time, the wild is the most calming place I've ever experienced. It's the best of both worlds. The month was filled with many "almosts"—a bull ducking my shot at just forty yards; calling another bull into just ten yards but unable to get a shot; sneaking up on two great bucks in my socks, needing just another ten yards to go, and having two hunters scare them off as they stood in the middle of the field at prime time. It was another year of learning and humbling from the wild animals we pursued and from Mother Nature.

And then it happened. Unexpectedly. Heart-wrenching. Healing.

CHAPTER THIRTY

As the archery season of 2021 ended, I felt an intense pull from the universe to escape back to the mountains, to be alone. I ended the relationship I was in and in doing so, I crushed his heart. I lacked the ability to show compassion because I felt lost and disconnected from myself. I remember this moment so vividly, and even the smell in the house.

It smelled like bacon while I held a cup of coffee in my hand. I was standing in the kitchen one morning, looking around at the comforts and conveniences I had around me. Out of nowhere, reality hit me hard. I wasn't happy with myself, with my relationship, and felt disconnected from my path in life. I needed to reconnect with who I was, and I couldn't do that while dating someone. I needed to be alone, to focus on why my intuition was telling me to run to the mountains. I needed space to clear my head and to dig in deep with the unhealed trauma from my past.

I knew I wanted to write this book, but every time I opened my computer to write, I stared at the white screen, unable to type. I was no longer working out, and everything important to me got put on the back burner. That day in the kitchen, it all came crashing down on me. The realization hit me hard, and to say I was confused is an understatement. My friends were surprised by my sudden breakup, and my partner fought for answers. Answers I didn't have. The feelings that hovered inside me only fed my insecurities as I started to doubt my decision.

My ringing phone brought me out of my trance. I got a call from Ben at Timber Bench Outfitters asking if I wanted to come guide for the third and fourth rifle season. I packed my gear into my truck and headed up the mountain.

Pulling off the highway onto the gravel road, my heart told me I was in the right place as I opened the gate and made my way up the bumpy and familiar road. Flashbacks from 2017 when I first stepped foot on this property brought a smile to my face and reassurance that I was right where I needed to be. The clarity was slowly starting to come back.

Hunting season commenced and it felt good to connect with clients again as I took on the role of lead guide. I fell into my natural stride of guiding and had a great season with a 50-percent success rate for my clients. I forgot how much I loved guiding, and it fueled the fire within me. Conversations regarding my taking over operations at Timber Bench Outfitters kept coming up, as Ben was looking to phase out and pass along the responsibilities to someone he knew would succeed. Over the past years, Ben would make comments about me taking over the place, but I never had the desire to. Not yet anyway—not until this year.

As I chatted with clients, they asked if I would return next year, and if so, they would love to come back and hunt with me. I informed them of the changes we had been discussing, and the support and encouragement were astonishing. It had my brain spinning, as I questioned my future path in life, and once again, the clarity became clearer.

Thanksgiving of 2021 was spent gutting and skinning an elk a client had shot. We celebrated the life of the elk and the new friendships around us with a glass of whiskey and a simple Thanksgiving meal. Sitting at the family table in the lodge, my hunting clothes were red with blood, and underneath my fingernails showed evidence of hard work, as they were stuffed with dried blood.

My heart nearly burst out of my chest as the energy in the room buzzed with life and the successes we all had. As the only woman in the hunting camp, I felt at home among the men, and they treated me no differently. The last night of the fourth rifle season approached, and my two clients were the only ones left in camp. They were an energetic duo and were happy to be going home with elk meat in their freezer. We sat around the dinner table and passed around a mason jar of moonshine, and laughter filled the room as we talked about hunting stories from the past. The next morning, they headed back to the West Coast and soon the mountain was quiet again.

I picked up my laptop and I started writing. For the next two weeks, I rarely left the cabin as the words seemed to flow out of me, my fingers couldn't type fast enough, and my untold story started to play out. I had been inspired by the men I hunted with and the success I had in the field. The snowy weather held me captive in my cabin as the wood stove brought a cozy feel to the healing I was conquering with each story. Healing can be a scary journey but, for once in my life, it was so natural and I no longer feared it but embraced it as I relived special memories from my childhood. I relived the scary ones too and realized that, without those traumatic moments in my life, I most likely wouldn't be where I am today.

I talk a lot about hunting and my connection to the wild in this book, and while I wrote about it, something clicked in my brain. I opened a new tab on my computer and wrote up a proposal to Ben and his business partner, Dean, regarding taking over management as well as booking and guiding hunts from our two remote cabins that back up to the National Park forest. I expressed my deep passion for guiding and how my life's dream has always been to run my own guiding operations, and now was the time to make that transition. But as a company that has been in business for twenty-five years, it was a gamble trusting me with such responsibility. I knew they believed in me, but I needed to prove to them that I wanted this and that I wouldn't allow myself to fail. Once again, the words seemed to flow like wine as I typed up my proposal and hit send. It was all or nothing, and soon I would find out what the verdict was.

It turned out Ben didn't sleep that night as he was blown away by the proposal I had sent that evening before. I had proven myself throughout the years guiding and, in that email, I poured out my heart, and Ben came to a decision. He realized it was time to hand over responsibility and was more than happy knowing I would be the one taking it over.

I spent the winter of 2022 up on the mountain at Timber Bench Outfitters headquarters with Tom the chef. Most of our days consisted of shoveling snow, hauling, and splitting firewood, and endless hours on the computer and phone, answering questions, responding to emails, and trying to get my upcoming season booked. My body and mind became shaped by the mountains that surrounded us and I found a new friendship in Tom, a fifty-eight-year-old mountain man.

With no running water besides the kitchen sink, life came down to the basics. I would bathe in the warm afternoon sun with hot water from the sink, standing on a couple sheets of wood so I wasn't standing in the snow. We had outhouses for bathrooms, resulting in many cold mornings on the throne, and we even had to heat our cabins with a wood stove. The dogs were able to run wild and free from a leash, and we constantly sought adventure. There was something so primal about being on the mountain and knowing if you wanted to stay warm at night, it would require time and work. Many weeks would go by, and we hadn't made it off the mountain.

Time slowed down living on the mountain, giving me the space to really focus on the last ten years of my life. So many changes, so many big moments and hurdles had been crossed that, for a long time, it all seemed to blend together. Being so disconnected from the world felt intoxicating as I broke down each year, each experience, and each phase as I went from a shy church girl to who I am now. The cold winter days were exactly what I needed, and it was almost as though I was being reborn—the cabin was my cocoon and come spring I would emerge, my wings ready to take flight.

I got back together with my ex in the spring, and I once again got a glimpse into his dark side later that summer when I told him I didn't like him smoking cigarettes. The look in his dark, glassy, beady eyes was unfamiliar and scary as he came storming into my cabin, throwing beers, his marijuana, and cigarettes at the trash can. I told him he scared me and he just laughed in my face. He proceeded to yell at me about how he wasn't good enough and how I was always trying to change him.

"Why can't you just love me the way I am? Is that too much to ask for?" he screamed at me, his body shaking. This wasn't the first time I had experienced him losing it when I confronted him about something, and I was ready to end the relationship then and there. Hearing his truck start and gravel fly, he squealed off the mountain without another word.

I was done, I was ready to end this relationship, or so that's what I told myself. He returned later that night exclaiming how much he loved me and how he needed to work on his reactions to situations such as this. As I listened, I asked him if he *was* sorry, because he never once apologized. It was all about himself and nothing about how he needed to work on regulating his emotions and finding healthy ways to communicate. I fell right back into his bullshit and told him the only way I would stay with him would be if he saw a counselor and stopped smoking cigarettes. He agreed he would, then never did. And yet, I stayed.

Growing up, I always told myself I wasn't worthy of love. That I wasn't pretty enough, skinny enough, or good enough. My body held the score, and this was a side effect of the sexual trauma I suffered, from being raised in a family where we were yelled at, spanked, and rarely received one-on-one time with our parents. This can have long-term effects on oneself and their relationships, and many times, people who have suffered abuse will often settle into relationships that are not healthy for them. Just like I did.

Sure, my ex and I had many great memories in the field, looking and hunting for elk, or fishing for trout on the rivers, but those traits alone cannot sustain a relationship and it won't last.

I longed for growth, as a couple and individually. I needed to be with someone who would inspire and push me every day, and I simply wasn't receiving that. I knew I needed to end the relationship and I thought if we put in the work, we could have the dream love life we all desire. I wasn't ready to give up, yet I was the one walking on eggshells. My body held the score, and I did what I knew best—I survived.

CHAPTER THIRTY-ONE

Taking over the management of the two remote cabins at Timber Bench Outfitters kept me busy through the summer with a list of chores. The cabins needed to be deep cleaned, as they were only used during the fall months. New lining for the counters and cupboards was installed, along with vacuuming and wiping down every surface, as the mice had called this home.

It felt good getting my hands dirty and creating a comfortable and clean space for our upcoming hunters. The showers outside needed some TLC, so I created a pulley system attached to a ten-gallon bucket that would hold hot water which would be gravity fed to a shower head. I even bought myself a chainsaw and fell in love with cutting down, hauling, and stacking firewood.

At one of the cabins, I created a food cellar/cooler in which I dug a giant hole and then placed the cooler in it. Building a frame around the cooler, I filled it with dirt, creating a natural cooling system for our food up at camp. Thousands of hours, sweat, and tears were spent at these cabins preparing for the season. My days were spent under the hot sun, and my muscles were proof of my hard work. I set up trail cameras and spent endless hours glassing. I wasn't going to fail my clients, and I'd be damned if I failed myself.

That summer, I learned a lot about myself, and when all my family except for me attended a family reunion, I was triggered. The nightmares came back, along with the emotional roller coaster. It broke my heart that I couldn't be there running around with my nieces and nephews, missing out on quality family time, especially since I had missed so much of it during the past several years. I was angry at myself for not being able to be around my brother, and I resented my family for not trying to include me. A heavy weight came over me as I hibernated in my cabin staring at the bottle of whiskey on my counter. Shame coursed through my blood, making me want to throw up.

I tried to talk to my ex about the issue, but he didn't have much comfort or really anything to say. A dark loneliness sank in, and there, with tears streaming down my face, I thought about killing myself. I thought about going far out into the forest and putting the barrel to my head. I just wanted all of it to end. I was tired of feeling, and I was tired of trying to fight. I had put in years of healing and self-work, and yet here I was choosing death over life.

I looked out the cabin windows as the warm sun glistened, and the aspen leaves danced in the breeze. I grabbed my boots, laced them up, threw on my pack, and did what I knew best: I headed for the mountain to find peace among the pines.

As I hiked up the narrow drainage, I followed a big set of fresh bear tracks. This bear had just come through here, I deduced as I stumbled upon a nearly steaming pile of scat. The foliage was thick and at any moment I could have bumped into the bear. I imagined what would happen if I surprised the bear as it napped or feasted on a meal. Stopping in my tracks, I feared what would happen if I did so. Death suddenly didn't seem so appealing to my depressive mind-set, and there on the mountain, I fell to my knees and wept. I had so much more to give to this world, more mountains to climb and sunrises to witness. I was not ready to leave this earth behind, and with shattering clarity, as a wave of self-worth came over me, I made my way back to the four-wheeler.

September was here, which meant it was the best time of the year. So much work had been done in preparation for hunting season, hoping everything would run smoothly and that we would find where the animals were hiding.

During the first week of the season, I had a one-on-one hunt with my client Kurt. He was my age, an avid hunter, strong, and healthy. He was ready to conquer whatever the mountain threw at us. Those five days hunting with Kurt will always be some of my best days in the field.

Opening morning, we got into the elk right at daylight, but a cow busted us, barking at us for nearly twenty minutes, letting every animal on the mountain know something was up. She couldn't smell us as we stood still on the old grassy road, being sure to not move a muscle, but could sense we were there. The day was hot and long as we sat next to a well-used water hole, seeing nothing besides a bear that needed a late morning swim.

Knowing there were plenty of elk on the other side of the valley, we were hopeful for the next morning. We parked the jeep and hiked to a scrub oak ridgeline and waited for just the slightest bit of light, then I let out a bugle. Instantly, I got a response just off to the south of us. We dropped in elevation so we could work with the thermals in our faces, toward the bull. As soon as we got to the bottom, another bugle blasted off above us and we made quick work of moving up the mountain to get set up. He was moving in quickly, clearly pissed off that there was another bull with his cows on his mountain.

I raked trees, made assembly mews, and challenged bugles, pulling the bull in just forty yards from Kurt. Kurt had ranged the only tree in front of him but when the bull stepped out, his shot went right over its back. Regrouping we heard another bugle from below us and were back in action. This bull was also pissed off that there was another bull on his side of the mountain and came just outside of range, screaming his face off at us. We never saw him, as he didn't want to commit, and soon it was quiet again.

We returned to camp for a late breakfast and a nap before heading back out. We knew exactly where we would hunt that night and ended up on the thickest game trail I've ever walked. As we crunched on sticks, I would cow call, trying to sound like a herd of cows feeding through. A small meadow lay below us, and soon a cow and a smaller bull presented themselves as they fed about. Meanwhile, the big bull from the morning let us know he was present with a challenging bugle, just off in the distance. Not being able to push forward due to the elk in front of us, Kurt decided to take a shot on the smaller bull sixty yards in front of him. It was nearly dark, and the elk started to feed back into the thick aspen grove. Kurt missed, knocked another arrow, took another shot, and missed again.

"It's better to miss them than wound them," I told him. Archery hunting is no joke, as only 10 percent of hunters are successful. Making an ethical shot under pressure at a moving target makes it even more difficult. Shooting at a target versus a live animal is completely different. Regardless, Kurt's attitude was positive, his mantra of "what's meant to be, will be" kept him pushing forward. I believe this mantra helped all of us on this hunt too. Morale can either make or break the hunt, and in this case, I believe it's one of the reasons why we found success on day five.

On day three, we got into a bugle fest with two big bulls down at the bottom of a steep, cliffed-out valley. They had acquired several cows and we watched them feed into the dark timber. We decided to hunt smarter and not harder, and planned to use an old, reclaimed road to get in above the herd bull that afternoon. That way, when he woke from his afternoon nap, we would be right on top of him.

At 5:30 p.m., I let out a bugle, and instantly, a scream came from below us. We quickly made a plan of attack, and just as we made moves to set up, the bull was already on top of us. When he saw our movement, he busted off. We tried to pull him back in but came up empty-handed. We spent the evening just up the mountain on a wallow, listening, hoping elk would come for an evening drink or that we could locate one. As soon as we backed out, we heard a bugle come from the mountain above us and had a focus for the morning.

Working our way back to the wallow we were at the night before, we located a bull above us, and bit by bit we moved in closer to him. The country we were hunting was made up of landslides in which one could make quick and easy work of moving up, but at the top of each, the benches were thick with ground cover, making it difficult to get in close without being too loud. As we worked this bull, I saw him on the skyline above, looking down at us, for the herd of elk we were pretending to be. When he didn't see any tan bodies and a set of antlers sticking up above the ground foliage, he walked off and went silent.

We worked the north side of the ridge following fresh tracks the entire way. We called and listened but turned up nothing, so we decided to head to the west side of the mountain where I had heard a faint bugle come from earlier in the morning. My body was tired as we side-hilled along the steep slide, and I even fell down a couple of times.

"You're getting tired, your steps are becoming lazy," Kurt said from behind me. He was right, I was exhausted and feeling slightly defeated.

Despite running on little sleep and many miles under our feet in just five days, we pushed onto the edge of the biggest slide on the mountain. Located at the bottom of this slide were cottonwood and tall fir trees along with aspen and willows. The erosion from the slide created a sandy floor that was cool to the touch. Later that day, we would name that spot "Kurt's Beach."

Taking a few moments to catch my breath, I blew a bugle into the basin below us. Not one or two or three but *four* bugles fired off within a few seconds of each other, the closest coming from just below us. All we had to do was move to the west of him, sneak downhill, and get on his level and piss him off. The wind blew every fifteen seconds and while it did, we made slow progress down the mountain, using the wind to mask our noise. It was the afternoon of day five, and I wasn't going to let this bull get away.

As we moved down the mountain, I cow-called, and each

time, we were reassured when a bugle kept coming from the same spot. Once we got on the bull's level, Kurt kneeled in some ground foliage just ten yards from me as I used a long stick to rake a willow bush. A broken bugle came from the bull, which I believe was from him standing up mid-bugle. Soon he, too, was raking a tree, and so I let out a couple of assembly mews, and within seconds, I saw Kurt pull his bow back, settle in, find his anchor, and shoot. There was no question about his arrow's impact as the sound of it hitting flesh echoed across the landscape.

The bull ran off another twenty yards but stopped as I let out a bugle. Hearing a groan and then a thud, the bull fell to the ground. The look of hard work, sweet relief, and success all at once came over Kurt's face as the reality of what just happened came upon us.

"What's meant to be, will be," I told Kurt as I gave him a big hug. "This hunt has been one I'll never forget, brother. This nearly tops it all." A feeling of pride and gratitude brought tears to my eyes.

We radioed a couple of guides from camp, letting them know an arrow was shot, and we had blood! Bull down! "Bring the water," we told them. "We've got work to do!"

The worst thing you can do as a hunter is shoot an animal and rush in before it has expired. This will only give a surge of adrenaline to these wild beasts, and they can run for miles. Climbing the hill, I radioed the guides to check in and heard crashing off to our left. Instant dread came over us, as we assumed I spooked the bull and he ran off, jacked up on adrenaline. We decided to give it another hour before going to look for him.

Two hours later, we finally decided to start following the blood trail, picking it up from where we last saw it. The blood was dark and filled with bubbles. A double lung shot, so we knew this bull couldn't have gone far. The ferns, grasses, and bushes were splattered in blood, and there was no shortage of it. Only having gone twenty yards from the shot, I looked up and saw the bull lying dead right in front of me. He had only gone forty yards in total before he fell over and died. The most ethical, humane way to put an animal down—no suffering as they quickly leave this earth behind.

Throwing my hand to my face in disbelief, I was ecstatic for our success and immediately gave Kurt a big hug!

"He's right there!" I exclaimed as I pointed at the bull just twenty yards away. Kurt had made a perfect, high, double-lung shot. But this bull had been laying in the sun for an hour now and we needed to get to work quickly before the meat would spoil.

A faint holler sounded from the beach as we hovered over the bull, our bloody hands quick at work, so I ran to the edge of the meadow and waved the guide over. The biggest smile covered his face as his eyes became glassy.

"Do we have a bull down?" he asked me in a tired and excited voice.

"You know it!" I told him. The three of us had worked so hard those five days, waking every day at 4:30 a.m. and hunting all day, and in bed no later than ten p.m. so we could get up and do it again the next day. We had many opportunities and did everything right, and finally, it all came together and the success we all shared was so sweet.

Just as we were about to finish, another guide, showed up to help us pack-out the hundreds of pounds of meat. Having chugged three beers on the way up, it didn't take long until he was lightheaded and couldn't carry the meat any farther. He was dehydrated and now the workload fell on us three. The day was hot, and we were sweating everything out as fast as we could consume it.

This meat needed to get on ice as soon as possible before it was ruined. The pack that the extra guide had brought up broke and now we had to carry this hind quarter out without one. What happened next was something I had been training for. During these moments one must do whatever it takes to ensure the meat gets back in a timely fashion.

Grabbing the massive hindquarter, I tossed it over my shoulder, the weight awkward, but I found a spot for it to settle in. I wrapped my arms up and around as much of it as I could and walked on forward. My legs were strong as they moved through the tall grass, up, around and over rocks and dead logs. The work it takes to carry these beasts off the mountain isn't easy, and it has a way of teaching us how to dig in mentally—to a place only hunting brings you.

We continued the pack out, our legs shaped by the mountain and the weight of this elk. Taking another break, we were all out of water and knew the hardest part had yet to come. What happened next gave me the ultimate respect for Kurt. He dropped his pack and met another guide just up the trail for some water. I offered to go get the water and felt competent to do so but Kurt insisted I take a break with the boys. You don't see this very often, if ever, in a guide situation. Kurt, you're a good man, and it was an honor to hunt with you. Perhaps another day we will make more hunting stories.

CHAPTER THIRTY-TWO

There was something that happened that first week of the season that I failed to mention in the previous chapter. Ultimately, what happened caused me to walk away from a company I had devoted thousands of hours, sweat, tears, and blood to. A company that downplayed every bit of what happened and tried to make me feel like the one who needed help, not the man who did me wrong.

After a warm breakfast of eggs, sausage, and potatoes, we shot our bows and ran through the afternoon plan. Spirits were high as it was only the second day of the season and the elk were just starting to rut. Kurt missed a bull that morning but remained hopeful for another opportunity.

I had sent my standby guide down to the main camp to grab ice for the coolers, and the thawed chicken for dinner that night. Upon returning, he told me of an uncomfortable and disrespectful comment another guide had made about me. One of our guides, who had frankly never hunted elk himself, was an older married man. He and I seemed to butt heads a bit, but I was cordial. Within the first day of knowing me, he had the audacity to tell me that Ridge Patrol would never succeed. He was that guy who would always have to one-up you in any conversation, as he tried to be the biggest man in the room. All the guides in camp also noticed this—he bragged about guiding big wigs and how he used to be on TV.

As my standby guide walked into the lodge that afternoon, he asked my guide, "Did Draya send you down to camp to grab her dildo for her?" The room was filled with clients, guides, the owner, and even his wife. Or that's what I heard anyway. Of course, later on, everyone's story about who was in the room was different and caused conflict within me on who to believe, ultimately making me realize I couldn't trust anyone within this company.

The weight and severity of this comment didn't sink in until the following week, as I was fully focused on getting Kurt a bull and staying at the remote cabin, away from the toxicity of it all. The clients I had the second week were snorers, and I am a light sleeper, so I stayed in the main camp for a good night's sleep and privacy. To top things off, my client blew his knee out on day two of his hunt, unable to walk much, forcing us to hunt the ground blinds on private land water holes. These changes put me back into staying at the main camp, and I could feel the toxicity there.

This seemed to piss off this pervert of a guide, as he left me a note in my jeep informing me I needed to talk to him first before putting a client on private land stands. The last thing I was going to do was talk to that creep. I couldn't even look at him without wanting to throw up or kick him in the balls. I brought the note to the men in charge at Timber Bench Outfitters and asked them if I had to report to this guide regarding stands on private land. This was in fact true. I told them that wouldn't happen.

Tears immediately flooded my eyes and rolled down my cheeks as I expressed to them what he had said about me the week prior. Ben acted completely surprised by this, claiming this was the first he had heard about it, but later I found out he was in the room when the comment was made. They informed me they would talk with him and that they respected my wish to stay clear of him. I told them that even if he apologized to me, I would respond in a way I didn't want our clientele experiencing. I was livid, I was violated and wanted nothing to do with the man, and if he dared to talk to me, there would be words and fists being thrown by me.

The following few days consisted of nausea and anger. I found myself hiding in the guide cabin, and a client even commented how I needed to smile more. His comment hit me hard, as I have always been a very smiley person—in fact, the most personable person at the ranch. The toxicity of the ranch was getting to me, and others were noticing. The fact that I was sexually harassed continued to be downplayed by nearly everyone with comments such as, "He had too many beers and made a drunk comment," "You're strong and you can't let what one person says about you affect you," that I was "being triggered from past trauma," and even a suggestion that I go find a therapist. I felt as though nobody had my back, that I couldn't trust anyone as they all had a different story, and overall felt a great amount of disrespect and support.

I packed up my essential archery gear and left everything I worked so hard for behind. Once I left, I was no longer welcome on the property, which was only validation that I had made the right move.

PART THREE

CHAPTER THIRTY-THREE

For those of you who don't know Ridge Patrol, I'm here to tell you we are so much more than just a clothing brand.

During the last week of September 2022, I ventured out with three girlfriends to hunt elk with our bow and arrows. That week of hunting was proof of the impact our clothing had made on these women. The confidence they carried with them as they faced each challenge was empowering. We had an absolute blast as we hunted a bull my brother had sent me in the direction of. The steep and insanely thick country made it hard to get in close but we sure as hell tried.

There, in the mountains of Colorado, our sisterhood deepened. The three ladies were new to hunting, especially calling elk, but we worked together to try and get this bull to come in close. We had him under one hundred yards several times, but unfortunately, we were never able to get a shot. Special memories were made in the elk woods as our patience was tested. I always thought, growing up, I would only hunt with my family, for spending time with those out of the church was treading too close to temptation. Turns out, I now have family everywhere that I know I can call on, if need be, especially these women.

There's something special about friendships with genuine women who don't use their "assets" to gain followers and likes on social media. The female hunter is one of the largest growing demographics today and we must stick together, support, and build each other up. We are the next generation of hunters. Let's lead by example and with humble hearts. Ridge Patrol may only have a couple years in the business world, but I am here to tell you we are not going anywhere. We have claimed our place in this industry, and we will continue to make clothing that compliments the outdoor woman, no matter what adventure she seeks.

CHAPTER THIRTY-FOUR

The hum of the highway had put me into a relaxed trance as I looked out the window of our van, my mind wandering as I got lost in the big sky, the golden fields of grass, and the endless mountain ranges. Our large family would soon be arriving at the Livingston Montana KOA for another family reunion. As my forehead rested on the cool glass window, I told myself that one day I would live here, that I would explore those mountains and run through the valleys; I would become a woman who ran with the wolves.

The gravel road was a welcoming sound as I made my way along the Ruby River Valley located just outside of Alder, Montana. With one hand on the steering wheel, my eyes were locked on the breathtaking view from my windshield. That spirit I felt as a young girl looking out that back window was still there as I drove down the windy road. My boyfriend at the time claimed to support my choice to come to Montana and guide for Upper Canyon Outfitters, but it didn't take long before I was leaving behind that relationship too, for I would no longer tolerate untrue and harsh accusations along with the lack of trust and respect. I would no longer be held back from pursuing my dreams, staying in a relationship I was not trusted in. I had a new slate and would soon find a family with the employees and clients as we guided elk and mule deer hunts. My life suddenly had a new trajectory, and my excited heart welcomed it.

All was quiet when I pulled up to the lodge. The guides were in town at a local bar, and I seized the opportunity to let my feet move underneath me, so off I went exploring the property I would be calling home for the next six weeks.

The evening sky was painted a gray-blue haze and just the slight subtlety of light pink. The cottonwood trees still held onto their bright orange and yellow leaves, and in the dim light they brought a pop of color to the valley I stood on. A steep mountain blanketed in dark timber, scattered meadows, and ridgelines brought up the backdrop to the wooden lodge. Looking around in awe, I felt small as mountains surrounded me in all directions. Taking a deep breath, I could feel an energy so powerful and grounding. The cool evening breeze snapped me out of the trance and with clarity, I knew I was right where I was supposed to be, and that life once again would bring change.

The grounds the lodge sat on were historically known as sacred grounds for the Shoshone Native Americans. Fighting and killing would not be tolerated here, as this was a place of peace and acceptance. I could feel this deep within my soul upon arriving here, and with each client I guided, they, too, were consumed in it. Having experienced sexual harassment at the previous outfitter along with the overall disrespect from the owners, and then going through a breakup filled with accusations, I knew I was going to be okay, as the energy those wild Native Americans created here warmed my heart and brought peace within.

During the first week of the season, I had the pleasure of guiding a woman who won the elk hunt through the Rocky Mountain Elk Foundation. As a new hunter, my client was ecstatic to be pursuing elk for the first time. At age fifty-seven and having asthma, it took her a bit longer to hike the mountains, but step by step she conquered each day. The first snowstorm dropped half a foot of snow, creating even more difficult conditions to navigate the steep mountains. After two days of low-hanging clouds and limited visibility, we welcomed the sunny blue skies.

After being hunkered down during the storms, the elk and deer were happy to feast, and they, too, soaked in the sunshine. Sitting on top of a ridge line we watched hundreds of elk feed out, calling as they went. Unfortunately, we could only shoot a cow on that particular piece of private property and overall, it was too far of a shot, so we decided to head back to camp.

As we made our way down the snow-blown ridge, a herd of elk headed our way from the dark timber across the ridge from us. They were four hundred yards away, too far of a shot for her, so we made quick work of closing off another hundred yards. A beautiful dark-antlered bull, with six points on each side, brought up the rear of the herd as they fed into a meadow just 250 yards below us. Setting her up on her shooting sticks, she tried to find the elk in her scope, which felt like it took forever, and finally, fired a shot, but missed.

"Rack another round!" I told her, as the elk were confused by what just happened. Taking two more shots and missing both, the elk ran off. A sign of frustration and a look of disappointment came over her face.

"Let's go confirm there is no blood," I insisted as I grabbed the shooting sticks and her rifle. I was confident she missed the bull but wanted to be 100 percent sure. The next day, we sat in the same spot and felt confident due to seeing the same herd bedding on the next ridgeline earlier that morning.

We spent the day under a tall pine tree, sitting around a small fire and connecting as women in the field. We talked about life, its hardships, and its triumphs. Time went by quickly and soon the temperatures started to cool off and the mule deer were up and feeding. We watched a mature four-by-four buck feed on a ridgeline roughly four hundred yards away. Soon more deer appeared below us at just 250 yards, as another buck pushed around his does.

My client set up her rifle on a tree branch and braced herself into the tree, holding the rifle snug to her chest. All we needed was for the buck to turn broadside for a shot. Looking over my shoulder, I saw another great buck walking the skyline, dropping down as he walked head-on toward us. Swinging her gun around, we waited for the buck to offer a shot. Once again, she pulled the trigger at one hundred yards and missed. Every deer on that mountain took off running and soon the mountain was quiet again. Feeling defeated and humbled we made our way back down the snowy mountain to camp. Sitting down at dinner, she informed me that she and her husband were going to leave in the morning. I tried my best to convince her to enjoy one last morning with me in the field. Sleeping on it, she sent me a message the next morning informing me she wanted to do so.

Getting settled in, we stood in front of a small spruce waiting for the big herd of elk to funnel in. Just after daylight, several bulls appeared on the skyline as they started to make their way down into the small valley, we were in. One by one the elk cruised by as my client tried to calm her excited nerves.

"Are you going to shoot one?" I asked her, worried our opportunity would walk on by. I informed her I would cow call to stop a cow in front of this particular bush. When she felt ready and if the elk was broadside, she should take a shot. Moments later, the morning air was blasted with sounds of rifle fire as the elk ran off.

"She's down!" I exclaimed as I jumped up and down. A perfect double-lung shot, a little high, causing the cow to fall and roll down the hill. A look of relief came over Sherine's face, for she had worked so hard and with persistence, not giving up until she was able to harvest a beautiful cow elk. She would go home with the best and cleanest meat out there to help feed their family, and a heart full of memories and pride.

The following week, I had the privilege of guiding a private land hunt for Dan and Lia. Dan had been hunting since he was eight years old, and his wife Lia was fairly new to the sport, this being her very first elk hunt. They had been training hard and shooting their guns often to be as prepared as possible for this Montana hunt, something we all should do when planning on going on a western hunt.

My week with these two hit me just a little different. I was humbled by their wisdom as they shared in detail their life stories with me—from a near-death experience to leaving an unhealthy marriage, to finding a love so pure. The energy was clearly working its magic as both Lia and Dan shot an elk that week. Lia harvested a healthy big cow and Dan a big six-by-six bull.

Just as the dawn broke one day, we sat there huddled in the buggy, our binoculars up to our eyes as we glassed for a bull elk or a nice mule deer buck. The high winds rocked the buggy back and forth, making it hard to hold steady. The dark sky to the north loomed in the background and soon was upon us. Unable to see anything, we cranked the heat, but it wouldn't work, so we layered up and waited out the storm. The snowstorm dropped a few inches and as it moved up the valley, it left behind low-hanging clouds on the mountains we were hoping to glass. Unable to see anything, I shifted the buggy into drive, and we headed down to glass the landscape below us. The heat finally started to work as we slowly crawled along the rocky roads.

Heading back to where we just came from, we descended into the valley. Bracing myself with the steering wheel and leaning back, I swiftly drove the buggy down another rocky road. We decided to get out and go for a short walk down an easy-going ridge.

"We'll go in light," I told Dan and Lia. Grabbing only the shooting sticks and my gps tracker, I led the way out.

Spot and stalk hunting has quickly become my favorite style of hunting and guiding. From reading the landscape, knowing where to look, playing the wind, going at just the right speed, and stopping to glass at just the right areas. As we slowly worked this ridgeline, the snow fell heavily, so we hunkered down under the big pine to wait for the storm to pass once again. As soon as it passed, we slowly crept to an opening so we could look down into a section of the north-facing hillside.

Bedding at the bottom, a six-by-six bull was taking a morning snooze. I instantly took a few steps back and whispered to my clients to be still and quiet. I ranged the bull at 250 yards, and he was laying at an angle with just enough of his vitals exposed to take a shot. All my senses were on high alert and we waited until the bull's eyes were closed for Dan to take a shot.

Stepping back out into the small opening and finding him in my binoculars, I knew it was time. Being so close to this bull, there was a chance the wind would switch or swirl, and with the slightest sniff of us, he would bolt and run. Dan and Lia both joined me as we worked as a team to get Dan set up for a shot. Lia held the shooting stick and I watched in my binoculars as Dan took his first shot. The shot echoed through the ravine, and I told him to rack another one. I could see the bull was hurting badly as he swayed back and forth. I instructed Dan to get ready, that the bull was currently behind a tree, and there was no shot. Patiently, we waited for the bull to move. Finally, he did and presented another shot. I cow-called to stop him and Dan placed a perfect shot directly into the vitals.

The special aspects that make up these hunts are not just the harvest but many times it's the hard work, the dedication, and pure ethics. Dan had been through a lot in life, nearly dying of cancer and miraculously surviving and dedicating his life to doing what's most important to him, one of those things being hunting. Dan had never harvested a bull elk before, making for an emotional success. Another hunt I'll never forget and am honored to be a part of.

The rest of the season was filled with more success and it just felt so damn good to be doing what I love most. The days got colder, and the wind didn't slow down, but my clients were troopers. Relationships were made on the mountainside, and just like that, five weeks of season was over. As the guides packed up their vehicles and traveled far and near to their homes, tears rolled down our faces as we had to say good-bye. We had all become so close during that short time, as we lived and worked together doing what we loved most.

CHAPTER THIRTY-FIVE

The howling and bitter-cold wind hadn't stopped blowing for multiple days now. The snow piled up on the front porch, and every few hours I bundled up and faced the wrath of the cold to shovel the snow. The cabin creaked as the gust came through with a vengeance. I often felt like the wild bears that roam these mountains, hibernating in my cozy oasis, only wandering out when necessary.

Some mornings we wake to blue skies, yet the wind prevails. The wind brings tales from the Shoshone Native Americans who used to occupy this valley, the perfect place to hang and dry their meat and hides in the relentless wind. I can feel their energy here, as they survived off this land, the warm springs just upriver creating a place to bathe in the middle of the winter. As I hike along the many ridgelines, I feel their spirit there too, as they hunted this land long before us, leaving traces behind in the shape of an arrowhead one may stumble upon here or there. The wildlife that thrives in this valley blows my mind as I daydream of the upcoming hunting season.

The closest town is forty minutes away, and I'm okay with that. Being tucked away from the chaos of the world keeps me connected with my roots. I've never been one for city life, as you have read. Wild places are where I thrive.

You never know who you're going to inspire, you never know how impactful your story may be to someone, you never know who will scoff at you or downplay what you have been through, but you can't let that hold you back. You must speak your truth no matter what that may be.

Deciding to leave behind the teachings of the LLC was one of the best decisions I've made in my life. Not that I believe those who practice that religion are wrong, but it simply wasn't for me. Spirituality is personal; we all find it in different places. When I chose to do what was right for me—not for anybody else—my life gained purpose and true happiness.

When you choose *you* first, beautiful life changes will happen. Chasing your passions is worth it, I can guarantee you that. There will not be growth without struggle and failure, which is easier said than done. I am the wealthiest I have ever been and that doesn't define my amount of money in the bank or materialistic goods—rather, I am rich in happiness, love, and growth. All because I chose me.

When I first started seeing a counselor, I was eager to tell my story and found I was having deep profound connections with others who had gone through some type of abuse. Several of those friends who confided in me told me how I was the very first person they told their truth to. I hope they are continuing the work of healing, and I thank them for being vulnerable with me. If you have suffered abuse of any type I am here for you. Please, reach out to me, you don't have to go through this alone.

I'm here to flip the script, to tell you to chase that passion that lights a fire under your feet, because when you do, you are limitless in what you're capable of doing. Surround yourself with people who lift you up and cheer you on as you climb that mountain, because a climb it's going to be.

A friend once told me, "Draya, life is like climbing a mountain. Some days are rainy and muddy, and with every step you take, you slip back. But some days, the sun shines warm and bright, and you make progress ahead." This message applies to all things—maybe it's your career, your healing, the hunts you venture on, relationships, or even your own demons. You don't have to hide from them anymore. Face them head on, and if you fall, then get back up again. I am here to cheer you on because I know exactly how you are feeling. Don't let your story hold you back—let it fuel your fire within. And parents, please educate your children and let each one of them know they don't have to say yes, they have the power to stand up for their boundaries, and they never have to touch anybody. Encourage your children to ask questions, and together, let's change this generational pattern.

And, so I ask you now, *What's your wild?*

In closing, I'd like to thank you all for taking the time to read *What's Her Wild: An Untold Story*. Now that my story has been told, I hope it brings more awareness to the healing powers that don't involve medications with serious side effects. I hope my story inspires you to heal from your wounds and that there is beauty in being vulnerable. You, too, can find the healing powers in nature, whether that means going for a hike, sitting by a stream, laying on your back and counting the stars—whatever it may be, Mother Earth is here for you. I am here for you. We are in this together.

Much love,
Draya

ACKNOWLEDGMENTS

I couldn't do this without you . . .

Completing this memoir hasn't been easy. It has taken me several attempts and years to complete, and I couldn't have done any of this without you. I want to give a shoutout to those who have made such a profound impact on my life. I wouldn't be where I am today without any of you, so thank you.

Annie McIntosh: You changed my life. You made me see the light I once knew as a little girl. Thank you for providing me the space to be vulnerable and speak my truth. When I was at my lowest and had nobody, you were there. You were my rock and you set my healing into motion. You are such a beautiful soul, and I am honored to have spent time with you.

Amy Waaraniemi: Hey, soul sister. We have been through some intense times together, and I wouldn't take any of it back. Thank you for allowing me the space to feel safe and heard when I told you about my abuse. Thank you for always being my sounding board, through all of it. You officially win the best roommate and friend award. I love you, and I am so proud to call you my sister.

Trevor Fredrickson: For the majority of my life I resented men, but then I met you. Thank you for picking up your phone that night I hit rock bottom. You played a vital role in my life when I was at my darkest, and when I started to see the light, you were there too. I hope this message finds you well, my friend. May your skiing lines down the mountain be filled with fresh powder in your face, and your laps down the river filled with adrenaline and peace.

Phoebe Larsson: What do you say to a person who has literally been through it all with you? Thank you for opening your home and business so I could have a place to not only live but to find myself. Those years at Whitewater are some of my favorites, and it was all made possible because of you. The memories we hold together are so special. I was so scared and unprepared for the world, but you were there, and for that, I am forever grateful. Thank you for always believing in me.

Ashley Mauldin: Your guidance through EMDR therapy changed my life. You helped give me the tools to recognize the trauma in my body, to listen to it, to feel it, and to let it go. Thank you for helping me reconnect with the young, carefree girl I once was.

ABOUT THE AUTHOR

Growing up in a family reliant on hunting, Andraya took to WILD places quickly as a young girl. First-time author, co-founder of Ridge Patrol clothing, professional photographer, and hunting guide, Andraya is here to share her story and hopes to inspire others along the way.

www.ingramcontent.com/pod-product-compliance
Lightning Source LLC
Chambersburg PA
CBHW052140070526
44585CB00017B/1902